Every Parent's Simple, Step

MW00978268

How to Raise a

SUPERCHILD!

Ray G. Strobel

and the staff of the
American Superchild Institute

Illustrations by Ekaterina Shulzhenko

Health Communications, Inc.
Deerfield Beach, Florida

www.hcibooks.com

**Library of Congress Cataloging-in-Publication Data
is available through the Library of Congress.**

© 2008 Ray G. Strobel
ISBN-13: 978-0-7573-0767-6
ISBN-10: 0-7573-0767-1

Publisher: Health Communications, Inc.
          3201 S.W. 15th Street
          Deerfield Beach, FL 33442-8190

R-08-08

Contents

Raising Your Child to Become . . .

Raising Your Child to Become
President!

Degree of Difficulty
5.5

As improbable as it may seem, if your child is a male you can forget the presidency. By the time he is fifteen or sixteen years old, we will have elected our first female President and will never look back. A male's only choice by then will be vice president, and we do not cover such mundane professions in this guide.

However, as with men, women candidates will still not require a high IQ or high moral standards, as we will continue to select the worst of us for our leaders. And that's good news for you as a parent. Raising your little Commander in Chief will not be difficult, as you will note from our Degree of Difficulty rating, which is only slightly higher than that of Bartender.

Cost of Upbringing	Income Potential	Cost/Income Ratio
$$$$	$$$$$$$$	**8.2** (1–10) Higher is better

Pros	Cons
Get your face on a stamp ⟶	Have to be dead first
Secret Service detail ⟶	Secret Service detail
200 million Americans (50%) will love her ⟶	Rest of world hates her
Go down in history ⟶	For even the stupid stuff
"Hail to the Chief" ⟶	Can't dance to it

Qualifications

An exhaustive analysis of the qualifications of each of the last seventeen presidents (the first twenty-six don't count since they campaigned prior to the advent of TV) shows conclusively that the requirements are:

1) Must be born in the United States and be a citizen
2) Must be at least thirty-three years of age
3) Must be breathing
4) Must be able to smile convincingly into TV camera*

---
* The sole exception to this rule was President Richard M. Nixon

As a parent seeking to raise a President, you might remark on how easy this is going to be (actually, it is), but remember, these are the four *main* requirements. There are many more little-known minor requirements that we will be revealing here for the very first time.

Because you will be privy to these, *your* child will succeed while others will fail (unless some other parents bought this book, too).

Follow these instructions to the letter, and soon you'll be schmoozing with prime ministers, dictators, kings, and sheiks—and sleeping in the Lincoln Bedroom.

3

Whatever you decide to name your daughter, her room should always be referred to as the Lincoln Bedroom (unless you've named her Lincoln, in which case you may refer to it as "her" room).

In any event, get it ready! Tack up the red, white, and blue bunting, and paint the presidential seal on the ceiling, where she can gaze at it from day one. A CD player will suffice to welcome her home from the hospital, but our best advice is to go with the complete 136-piece band grandly playing "Hail to the Chief"!

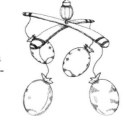

In the cradle
- Stuffed toys: donkey and elephant. None for Independents. She'll learn early why they never win.
- Hand-stitched Homeland Security blanket

On the mobile
Balloons: Red, white, and blue. Hanging from ceiling, ready for "spontaneous display" every time she burps

In the toy box
- 1:164 scale model of Air Force One
- Toy hotline
- Toy doomsday nuclear suitcase

Architectural addition
Major drywall work is needed to turn square room into more appropriate oval

On the wall
When she's still too young to declare: • Framed, autographed photos of Lincoln (R), Roosevelt (D,) and Nader (I)

The Teen Years
Emphasizing Evasiveness

When most parents ask their teenager a question they expect a direct answer. Resist this urge! Teach your little Commander in Chief the art of the evasive answer. It will serve her well.

"Did you finish your homework?" is a simple enough question, but a "Yes" or "No" answer is an early indication that your parenting skills are lacking. Trust us, she won't make it past the primaries with that technique. Once she starts answering with "That depends on how you define 'finish,'" you will know you're making headway.

When asked whether she has cleaned her room as requested, a winning answer might be along the lines of "Can we move past some of the debates around which we disagree and can we start talking about the things we do agree on?"

Home Tutoring

Fund-Raising
Although most of the subjects taught in school will be useful, one subject will be missing from the curriculum and will be key to her electability. Therefore, it will be your responsibility to teach her both basic and advanced fund-raising techniques. Some Clinton biographies are a good place to start.

Geopolitics
Since your daughter will be starting and waging wars once she grows up, it will be necessary for her to learn about the ten most powerful countries, economically and militarily, of her generation. School will not be of much help here because it will be teaching American history. In preparation for the year 2048, she must be immersed in the history, culture, and languages of China, India, Pakistan, Iran, Israel, Russia, Saudi Arabia, and France.*

* France will most certainly not be much of a powerhouse, but Paris will still be a great place to visit.

5

The Teenage Years—The Right Stuff

A good start to her winning ways will be when she is voted *President of Her Class* and *Most Popular* in high school. To ensure that success, your home must become "the 'in' place" to hang out. Plan for lots of all-night pizza parties. Remember, the key to everybody's liking her is that they like you, too. Be the parents all the other kids want for their own. Give them whatever they want. The fewer rules the better. They'll love you (and her) for it. She'll learn an important lesson when she discovers that people who like her will vote for her even if she has to buy their affection. Here's what they should find when they come over to visit.

On her computer
- Social Security numbers and all the dirt on all of her friends, family, and classmates
- Historical clips of the Kennedy-Nixon debate and the Clinton impeachment hearings

On her game machine
- Battleship!
- Grand Theft Election
- Risk

In her closet
- A multitude of flip-flops. It's important for her to embrace the concept early in life.

ELECT

SUE 2048!

On her wall
- Customized election poster goes up when she turns sixteen. Stays up through high school and college and beyond until the "big day."

In her cell phone directory
- *New York Times* political editor
- Speed dial to all 345 members of Congress
- A good lawyer

Necessary Character Traits for Your President-to-Be

As a parent, it is your job to make sure that your child develops certain critical character traits and to nurture important attributes that will be necessary to her becoming Commander in Chief. Many traits will, of course, not be necessary and could even hinder your child's quest for the presidency. Others—deceptiveness, for example—are essential. Refer to the checklist below to make sure that you place the proper emphasis where it belongs.

Competitiveness	✔	Neatness			Vindictiveness	✔
Compassion		Honesty			Deception	✔
Evasiveness	✔	Sense of humor			Narcissism	
Creativity		Cleanliness			Blame shifting	✔
Duplicitiousness	✔	Sympathetic			Industriousness	

Presidential IQ Factor
Is it really 1,028?
Is it true? Yes. The presidential I.Q. is really 1,028. Rigid scientific study has added the IQs of the last twenty-two presidents and come up with an exact total of 1,028. An astounding average of 46. This is why your child has a shot. (Of course, she would have an even better shot at the presidency of France, where the average is -14, but that's a different story.)

The problem is, you can't simply ask your child to cheat on her IQ test (even though that does show the right kind of initiative) because, well, her IQ would, in reality, still be too high. The solution is to stifle her academic and intellectual growth through excessive intake of trans fats and beaucoup de soft drinks, too much TV, and cover-to-cover reading of *People*. In other words, she should lead the typical American childhood.

Family Chores
Think about it for a moment. It's obvious, isn't it? Which family chores will best prepare your child?

Of course there won't be many (after all, the President won't be doing much real work). She should get used to having others do her work for her (it's called delegating).

Your little one should be in charge of calling all family meetings, which shall be called summits. This shall be done many times per day.

As far as lawn work is involved, ladies don't use lawn mowers, no matter what the feminists say. Her work should be concentrated in the rose garden.

Allowance

You're lucky here. No need for an allowance. Like the queen of England, the President carries no cash. If you give her an allowance, she'll get used to reaching into her pocket or purse and actually paying for something. This, plus the fact that there's no need to send her on for an advanced degree, is going to save you a bundle.

Veto Power

The difficult part of raising your little President will be the family rule that states: *every* family decision must be put to a vote. She must have the veto, of course, and that's where the problems come in. When she's young, for example, she'll veto your dinner menu suggestions and you'll all be eating PB&J seemingly forever. But stick with it.

You're just about done! There are, of course, some of the typical child-rearing techniques yet to practice. Yes—even

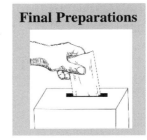

Final Preparations

though you have accomplished the difficult parts of raising your little Commander in Chief, there's still some work ahead.

Discipline, understanding right from wrong, ethics, honesty, etc., must be instilled, but these basics are generally taken care of in our excellent public schooling system. In any event, they're not really that important for this job.

It is the helpful hints we have given you here that are crucial. Missing one step can be costly.

Raising Your Child to Become a
Bestselling Author!

Degree of Difficulty
5.0

Don't want your child to grow up to be some flashy Rock Star? Just rich and famous will do? Well, here's the plot: you're going to have to work on character development.

You have a difficult assignment ahead of you. Not only will your child have to learn how to *read*, but to actually *write* as well. And don't confuse mere *author* with *bestselling* author, or your child may grow up depressed that nobody wants to read his works (or worse yet, he gets discovered only after he's dead—and who wants that?!).

Cost of Upbringing	Income Potential	Cost/Income Ratio
$$	$$$$$$$$$	**9.6** (1–10) Higher is better

Getting Started

As mentioned, you're going to have to make sure your child actually knows how to read *and* write. And that's no easy task in today's educational environment. You certainly won't be able to count on your local school, so home tutoring is a must. On the plus side, your child won't have to learn to write *well*; he is striving to become a *bestselling* author, not necessarily a *good* one.

Anyone can write a book. The trick is to find a publisher that will actually agree that your manuscript is publishable. Of course, then comes the really tricky part: getting the public to actually *buy* your book so you can make some money. And finally, the most important part: getting people to buy your books *while you are still alive* so you can enjoy the fruits of your labors (?) and spend that pile of royalties.

Sound daunting? Not to worry. We'll help you teach your budding Author-to-Be not only plot development, but also *hackneyed* plot development, and he'll be well on his way to royalties that would impress even J. K. Rowling!

Items such as a typewriter and yellow pads might be antiques, and look like mere clever decor, but they actually will help infuse your infant with "writer's vibes." Best of all, they will be useful later in life as props. Pretending to use them will help shape your child's image as an iconoclastic writer, which will be good for publicity and good for sales.

On nightstand
• Antique Underwood typewriter, yellow pads

In the toy box
• All *Peanuts* and *Garfield* cartoons, tons of comics (except Classic Comics), most pop-up books

On the wall
• Framed autographed photo of Robert Ludlum (boys), J. K. Rowling (girls)

Daily Activities

The Importance of TV

While most intelligent parents are desperately trying to limit the amount of time their children spend in front of the TV watching mind-less drivel, parents of a Bestselling Author-  to-Be are well-advised to do the opposite.

Of course, not just any old TV shows will be of help to their literary development. BBC-TV and PBS should be strictly avoided. Instead, we recommend sitcoms (*Joanie Loves Chachi* is especially recommended), action-adventure series (you can't beat *The Six Million Dollar Man*), as well as most American films from the '60s and '70s. These will help him gain a better understanding of complex plot devices and rich character development. Eight hours a day is minimum. Remember, your child will not be writing classics; rather, he will be churning out "bestsellers," the written equivalent of a bad sitcom or B movie.

Home Tutoring

Bedtime reading will be your major focus throughout his early and teen years. By the time he is thirteen or fourteen years old, it is hoped he can read for himself.

Recommended Reading
One through six years
- All *Peanuts* and *Garfield,* comics (except classics), most pop-up books

Early Teen Years
- All Jacqueline Susann
- All Tom Clancy

Before He Sells His First Short Story
He needs to be able to read and understand a publisher's contract and royalty statements, and hone his negotiating skills.
- *How to Negotiate Almost Anything*
- *The Art of the Deal*
- *Breaking Contracts for Fun and Profit*

Practicing Perfect Penmanship
The Importance of the Proper Scrawl

Since your child's works will be printed in book form, you may think neat penmanship is unnecessary. You would be wrong, of course, which is why you purchased this valuable manual.

Autographing his books will become a big part of your child's life, and perfecting the proper style for his signature is crucial. A neat signature is the sign of a boring person, and your child will want to be perceived as a bold, exciting genius. Since his autograph will be in great demand, speed is also a requirement. Make him work on his autograph early in life, and make him practice, practice, practice. Trust us, it will pay off.

Example A: Okay in grade school but too boring for your Bestselling Author-to-Be.

Example B: Getting there. Note the middle initial. Very literary.

Example C: Still needs practice. Looks messy, not creative.

Example D: Excellent, indecipherable scrawl. Shows genius; built for speed.

We have tried to make it clear why it is important that your child not write serious works of literature. The sad fact is, most Americans won't read them, and your little author will end up in the poorhouse. As the chart below shows, royalties are one thing, royalties *in the author's lifetime* are another.

Writers of "pop" fiction and non-fiction catch on quickly, hit the best-seller lists, and immediately start raking in the dough. If you've followed our advice, your little one might pen the next *Harry Potter* series when he's still in his teens (and since he would be under twenty-one, you would control his finances. Wouldn't *that* be nice!).

More "serious" authors, however, can see their works hang around for decades before the public decides they're worth the smallest bit of struggle to read and understand them.

Trust us. If you catch your little one reading Brontë, Solzhenitsyn, or Proust, steer him gently toward the TV. There might be a rerun of *Gilligan's Island* playing.

Don't Die Too Early

Royalties

Author	Title	Books Sold	Income*
Dan Brown	*The Da Vinci Code*	80 million	Lots of millions
Robert Ludlum	Various thrillers, including *Bourne* series	210 million	Mega millions
J. K. Rowling	*Harry Potter* series	Gazillions	Gazillions
Shakespeare	Various	Millions	Truppence
Charlotte Brontë	*Jane Eyre*	Tons	Ounces
Jack Kerouac	*On the Road*	Lots and lots	Little

* In the authors' lifetime, so they could spend their royalties

Even though your child will be getting rich turning out drivel for people who don't know the difference between Proust and *Peanuts* (and who think a dust jacket is something you wear while cleaning), it will be important for his self-esteem to be viewed as an important cultural figure.

Require that he memorize incomprehensible phrases from major literary works so he can drop them into conversations at will. Speaking of Proust, some of his lines will do just fine, and it won't be difficult picking out the incomprehensible ones. Old English lines from Shakespeare are always a good choice, too.

We guarantee that this training will help build your child's self-esteem as well as allow him to travel in celebrity circles.

Many Hollywood celebrities and Manhattan mavens like to include authors in their exclusive circles of friends, and your precious little one will do just fine with a combination of drivel coming out of his pen and profundities out of his mouth.

Raising Your Child to Become
Pope!

Degree of Difficulty
8.7

It's one thing to be able to address your child as "Mr. President," but to be able to slap him on the back and say, "Hey, kid, how's the *Holy Father* doing?" Now that's a trip!

Talk about exclusivity! Nowadays, everyone's a superstar or a billionaire, but there have been less than *fifty Popes* in the last *500 years*!

If you want your child to ascend to the Earthly Throne, some simple preparation is in order (naming him Leo will improve your chances, and a few specific child-rearing techniques are necessary). Follow our instructions carefully and someday you will be blessed with your very own infallible child.

Cost of Upbringing	Income Potential	Cost/Income Ratio
$$	$	**-2.2** (1–10) Higher is better

The Early Years

The major drawback to raising your child to become Pope is the long waiting period. It's not a case of his reaching adulthood and *poof!*, he's suddenly Pope, as would be the case if you had decided, for example, to raise a professional wrestler. No, he—and you —have a long wait ahead. On the plus side, it's a pretty plush job once he gets installed in office.

Also on the plus side, this lengthy "incubation" period is not all your responsibility. The Catholic Church will begin to be of assistance as soon as your child reaches school age, and will virtu- ally take over once he is old enough to attend seminary. Therefore, although you have to wait a long time, you'll have to work hard at your parenting for only a few short years.

Following are all the tips and techniques you'll need. Adhere to them religiously to reach your goal, and you will not be disappointed. And *keep the faith!*

Parenting Techniques

Let's first get the obvious out of the way. If your family is not presently Catholic, you are well advised to convert. Trust us, this will be of immense help.

Naming Your Child

Choosing the proper name for your Pope-to-Be is crucial. Thirteen popes have been named Leo, more than any other, so this is a good place to start. Sure, you could always name your kid P. Diddy, and he could take the name Leo when elected, but our research has shown that children given the proper "Pope name" at birth have a tremendous head start. And who wants to change his name that late in life, anyway? You know, the mono-grammed towels and all that stuff.

Recommended Pope-to-Be Names:

- Leo
- John
- James
- Peter
- Benedict
- Boniface*
- Agapetus*
- Innocent*

*Although these are legitimate Pope names, you might wish to consider something more traditional for your child, or he'll constantly get the crap beat out of him in gym class. Or worse.

Names Not Recommended

- Lefty
- Rocky
- Diablo
- Adolf
- Bruiser
- Atilla
- Bubba
- Butch
- The Pope formerly known as Prince

When he finally becomes Pope:
What's in it for you?

Aside from the awesome brag-ging rights, there isn't much in it for you. Sure, you get free trips to Italy on Air Vatican, but the guest wing of the Papal Palace is cold and drafty, so you'll proba-bly want to spend most of your time in downtown Rome.

The real bummer is, since Popes generally don't get elected until they're in their "twilight" years, you'll probably be dead by the time the little one finally ascends to the throne.

When your precious Pope-to-Be arrives home from the hospital, you will want to have his nursery prepared in the proper manner. As he rests comfortably, he must be surrounded by the proper Pope prompts.

Even though Popedom is probably more than seventy years away, you can never start too soon with proper parental guidance. This is a mistake many parents make. It's important to build "Pope drive," so that by the time he's walking, he's blessing everyone in sight.

In the cradle
• Stuffed toys: lamb, fish
• Bedding: straw
• Rattle that dispenses holy water

Baby's rattle

On the wall
• Framed, autographed photo of Jesus

Architectural additions
Bust out those walls! Balcony allows you to display child to neighbors and helps him get used to the adoring throngs . . .

. . . and more walls! For that stained-glass window (bought on eBay)

On the mobile
• Assorted antique crosses

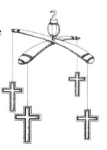

In the toy box
• Twelve disciples collectible trading cards
• Toy manger set
• Matchbox Popemobile

Designer vs. Swaddling Clothes

One of the major benefits of selecting Pope as your child's profession is the very reasonable cost of raising the future *His Eminence*. No costly wardrobe is necessary. In fact, it could be a roadblock in the future when "life of poverty" becomes a major consideration. Therefore, while your friends are mortgaging their futures roaming the aisles of Neiman Marcus in search of the latest trendy brands and logos, you can be content with shopping at the nearest resale shop. Don't worry if people "tsk, tsk" your little prince or if he is teased at school. This will only be temporary. The payback comes later when his peers are all begging for forgiveness for sins they don't even know they committed.

Potty Training

Although men don't normally start referring to the potty as *the throne* until late teen years, it is wise to begin referring to it as such early in the life of the future *His Eminence* to help him get used to the idea. After all, he will be sitting on one for even longer periods of time than most men his age. Care should be taken, however, so as not to confuse the little tyke, or it could prove embarrassing later in life.

Home Tutoring

When the little tyke is growing up, you can skip the math tutoring, but these areas need your help:

Vocabulary

- "Merry Christmas" in 147 different languages
- "Bless You" in 147 different languages
- Latin, Latin, Latin! Unfortunately, you will have to learn it, too!

Recommended Reading

How to Be Pope: What to Do, Where to Go Once You're in the Vatican by P. Marchant

Required Reading

The Cat in the Hat by Dr. Seuss

It Seems Like an Eternity: Raising Popes for Fun and Profit by M. Watt

---

How to Make a Proper Paper Pope Hat

Getting your little loved one to become accustomed to wearing the papal crown is easy when play is involved. Here's an activity that parents and children can do together. Follow these simple instructions and turn the Sunday funnies into a colorful replica of the crown he will one day wear. This is the sort of subliminal child-rearing technique that can make the difference between "possible Pope" and "Pope-to-Be." *For a complete how-to video demonstration, see YouTube.com/niftypopehat.*

Step 1. Take a double newspaper page and fold in half.

Step 2. Fold flap B over flap C and flap G alongside flap X, as shown.

Step 3. Cut along dotted line and make final folds, cuts, and creases.

Step 4. Unfold quickly, and it's a miracle—the perfect proper Pope hat!

Shown: Incorrect folds can result in an inaccurate representation of hat. Try again.

The Teenage Years—Keeping a Close Watch

It is very important to constantly monitor your Pope-to-Be's room for unacceptable, un-Popelike materials and to be on the lookout for any signs of un-Popelike activities. Remember, he still needs your guidance to keep him on the straight and narrow during this dangerous time in his upbringing.

The teen years are a crucial period when it can be easy to be led astray. Be vigilant!

On the computer
- Last website visited: Fodor's Sightseeing Guide to Rome
- Last Google search: "Virginity"
- Social networking site: www.popester.org

On the game machine
- Christian Founders: 3D Adventure
- Interactive Parables (Not recommended: Grand Theft Auto: San Andreas, Immortal Kombat)

Reading materials
- *Pope Illustrated*
- *Holy Bible* (check religiously for dummy covers)

On the wall
- Autographed poster of current Pope *(check underneath weekly for possible Pamela Anderson* Baywatch *poster. Movie poster from* The Exorcist *is acceptable)*

In the trophy case
- 1st place, Latin Speed Spelling

Final Preparations

You're just about done! Between the late teen period and the tense wait through the puffs of white smoke wafting over the Vatican conclave, there's really not much more to do—but to wait. And wait and wait.

During this time, you will, of course, be performing the usual child-rearing activities. Yes—even though you have accomplished the difficult parts of raising your Pope-to-Be, there's still some work ahead.

Discipline, understanding right from wrong, ethics, social skills, honesty, etc., must be instilled, but these basics generally take care of themselves, as any parent will tell you.

It is the helpful hints we have given you here that are crucial. Missing one step can be costly. For example, many parents, in hindsight, confess to not making enough paper Pope hats.

What About Sainthood?

Consider that you may spend all this time and effort to get your little one into the Vatican and suddenly realize it's not enough. So get working on those miracles now! You'll need at least one solid one to achieve that even more elusive goal: sainthood!

The teenage years are the best time to prepare. Teenagers are capable of all kinds of miraculous behavior—when they actually obey you or decide not to do drugs, for example. Therefore, it's important to keep a detailed diary of your child's formative years, documenting any actions that may be construed to be miraculous by future generations.

History has shown that raising people from the dead or turning water into Cabernet is no longer necessary. A simple good deed, if performed with a pure heart, may qualify, since, at the rate at which such actions are disappearing, twenty years from now it surely will be looked upon as miraculous behavior.

Raising Your Child to Become the
Mars Mission Commander!

Degree of Difficulty
8.8

Here's everything you'll need to give your child "The Right Stuff." If you regret not having done something exciting with *your* life (like discover America, for example), here's your chance to see your kid go where no man has ever gone before—unless the Chinese get there first. And if you get tired of her hanging around the house even into adulthood, here's the perfect way to get rid of her for a while (it can be an eleven month round-trip).

Ready? What are you waiting for? Get yourself into warp drive and follow our instructions carefully.

Cost of Upbringing	Income Potential	Cost/Income Ratio
$$$	$$$	**4.6** (1–10) Higher is better

28

In the Beginning

Get ready, this is going to be a blast! First you must prepare yourself for the fact that you won't be seeing much of Junior once it's time to suit up. The time it takes to travel to Mars depends on the distance between the two planets at the time of launch and on the speed of the spacecraft, etc. All this space jargon means is that your child will be gone for as little as six months and as long as eleven months at a time. This does not include the time spent on the planet's surface.

The good news is, by the time she's old enough to take off, the global warming will have progressed to global hotting and she will be looking forward to months in a climate-controlled spacecraft. In fact, by the time she returns, it will be hotter here, so she will probably sign on immediately for another tour of duty. But don't sweat it, you'll see the little one for two or three weeks a year.

Diet

One of your major parenting concerns will be your child's diet. Although it doesn't seem logical, she'll have to watch her weight. This is because, even though everything in space is weightless, chubby little Commanders still have to fit through those space locks. But lucky for you, watching her diet means you're not going to be spending lots of time in the kitchen preparing gourmet meals. In fact, that would be detrimental to her training. Better she get used to the microwave and reheated leftovers.

Saving leftover toothpaste tubes however, is exemplery—stuffing them with Wisconsin cheese and other gooey items will allow your little one to practice squeezing her meals.

The Early Years—Preparing Your Mission Commander-to-Be's Room

A place for everything and everything in its place. That's your mantra in setting up your child's room. Space will be at a premium in space, so get her used to tight quarters with everything stowed neatly. The room needn't be large; if an extra bedroom isn't available, a closet will do just fine.

DVDs for the player
- *2001: A Space Odyssey*
- *War of the Worlds* (*not* the Tom Cruise version!)
- *Apollo 13*
- *The Red Planet*
- *Star Trek* (the complete series)
- Tons of video games!

Wallpaper
Repeating pattern of Earth as viewed from outer space. Get her used to this perspective

On the mobile
- Planets of the solar system

In the toy box
- Erector Set
- Stuffed toy dog (Lakia)

On the wall
- Autographed poster of Captain Kirk
- Framed photograph of Yuri Gagarin

Home Tutoring

Your child will get all the math and science she needs in school, but she'll just turn out to be some dorkey scientist sitting back at Mission Control unless you teach her self-confidence and the ability to take command. So get to work.

In addition to the required reading listed below, some crucial vocabulary will need to be taught.

Required Reading
Edgar Rice Burroughs
H. G. Wells
Michael Crichton
Arthur C. Clarke

Specialized Vocabulary
"Roger Wilco"
"Over and out"
"Hey, I'm upside down!"
"Can you hear me now?"

The Early Years

All children need a time-out now and then when they get too agitated or unruly. When it's time for you to discipline your little Commmander-to-Be, you can kill two birds with one stone. She'll get a little quiet time, and so will you. Instead of sitting her in a corner or banishing her to her room, we recommend placing her in a dark closet for a few hours (as she grows older you can extend this time to as long as a month). Don't worry. She'll get used to the isolation, which will serve her well in later years in the blackness of space. And when your friends brag that they got a few minutes of relaxation during a time-out, you can one-up them with, "A few minutes? I get a whole month at a time."

Changing Diapers

Your friends will be aghast. But when your little Commander-to-Be poops in her pants, you'll casually say, "I'll change her in a few hours. It will do her good to wait. It's for her own good."

And it *really will be* for her own good.

So while all your friends are carrying diaper bags and cases of talcum powder, you'll be traveling light, with nothing but your iPhone. And your little one will thank you a few years in the future when she's on that twelve-hour space walk and the mission specialist asks, "Can you stay out there a few more hours?"

"No problem," will come the reply, "I've done this since I was six."

Stimulating Childhood Activities

A Fun Game for Your Commander-to-Be

It may seem like common parental advice when we recommend playing catch with your child, but you'd be surprised how few parents realize what great preparation for weightlessness this can be. Just make sure when you throw your child to your spouse, the trajectory is a high arc so your little Commander-to-Be has sufficient time to spin and flail about before being caught.

Back and forth. Back and forth. She'll scream with delight and be better prepared for her time without the gravitational pull of Earth.

As we said, few parents think of this.

The Opposite Sex

You're lucky! Most parents are traumatized by the problems of raising adolescents and teens when it comes to their attraction to the opposite sex. Makeup, muscles, pimples, puberty, and dates to the prom. Whew!

Well, *you* won't have to face those problems. With space suits, not only can't you tell who's attractive, but you also can't tell who's who or what's what. And anyway, with twelve people in a pod for six months, everyone starts to look good. So you'll save money on all those beauty aids. But don't skimp on the deodorant!

The Early Teen Years

Here comes what will seem like the difficult part of raising your little Commander-to-Be: it is crucial that she be the most likable kid in school. This is not to say the most popular, just the most likable.

It's obvious, isn't it? If you're going to be trapped in a pod for six months at a time, you will want to be with people everybody really likes. Likable people will also help avoid those inevitable in-flight fights; therefore, this attribute will help her be chosen not only as a member of a long spaceflight crew, but as the Commander as well.

So how do you go about raising your child to be so likable? It's not difficult, really. When they're young, being likable means the boys should be able to make farting sounds with their armpits and the girls will have to do whatever girls do to be likable. Of course, the real key will be her ability to tell jokes. Not just any jokes, but really funny ones, like "Why did the astronaut cross the universe?"

One
Million
Funny
Jokes

Actually, the most important reason likable people are chosen for interplanetary crews is in case they encounter Martians or other strange, extraterrestrial life forms. If Tom Cruise had been more likable, millions of lives could have been saved.

Early Adulthood
You may start to wonder about your choice for your child's profession when she turns inward and begins sitting in darkened rooms, staring into space. Don't despair. This is just proof of your superb parenting techiques. She has begun contemplating the universe in preparation for her first voyage. And fondly remembering her childhood time-outs.

Raising Your Child to Become a
Mega Billionaire!

Degree of Difficulty
7.6

Nowadays, multimillionaires are a dime a dozen. And the way the ranks of billionaires are growing (900+ at last count), by the time your child is twenty-one, he or she is going to need not one, but *lots* of billions. No problem!

How, you ask, can you guarantee that your child will grow up to be a billionaire when you haven't even figured out how to meet your mortgage or pay down your credit cards? The answer is that your parents (as loving and nurturing as they were) didn't start preparing you *at birth*. If you had been able to recite your IPOs when you were three, instead of just your ABCs, perhaps you would have bought Intel at twelve instead of that Internet flash-in-the-pan you bet your life savings on. So let's get started. The future dividends are worth it!

<u>Cost of Upbringing</u>	<u>Income Potential</u>	<u>Cost/Income Ratio</u>
$$$	$$$$$$$$$$$	**9.8** (1–10) Higher is better

Proper Names

Common sense tells us that names like Benson or Brooks would be helpful, but studies have shown otherwise. As it turns out, just any old name will do. After all, your Billionaire-to-Be will have about $350,000,000.00 in his college fund by the time he's twelve. Nobody's going to tease him about his name; everyone will want to be his friend! You can name him Boffo, if you want. And her, Hermionie. So let's move on to more useful parenting tips that will ensure his or her success.

The Allowance Quandary

Again, common sense is misleading. One would think that a child should be given a small allowance when he reaches ten or twelve to teach him the value of a dollar.

Your Über Child should be given spending (and investing) money before he can crawl. Watch how quickly he develops an early love for the stuff. By the time most other children get their first quarter from the Tooth Fairy, yours will understand the value of a dollar (and yen and euro and dirahm and yuan). He will be giving *you* an allowance before he reaches first grade.

Understand that a desire for all kinds of currency and valuable goods should be instilled early in his life. Know that Rolexes are for millionaries. Instead, give him an F. P. Journe for his fifth birthday, if not before.

The Early Years—Preparing Your Billionaire-to-Be's Room

Get that room ready! Money, money, money . . . that's the decorating theme that will jump-start your little dividend. Surround him with the symbols of wealth he will someday come to expect as his rightful due.

In the cradle
- Lifetime subscription to *The Robb Report*
- Twenty years' worth of Berkshire Hathaway annual reports
- His own Black American Express Card

The initial sign that you have successfully accomplished your task is when the first words out of his mouth are not "Ma-Ma" and "Da-Da" but "buy!" and "sell!"

In the toy box
- Monopoly game
- 99.9999 gold ingot
- Game of Risk

On the mobile
- U.S. and foreign currency in various (large) denominations (*He will recognize the portraits on the bills before he recognizes his grandparents.*)

On the wall
- Framed, autographed photo of William Buffett and reproduction of *Forbes* magazine's "Richest People in the World" list

Home Tutoring

Although your local school may be excellent, it's up to you to concentrate your child's education in the areas of finance and investments (sadly, these areas are missing from first–third grade curricula). This is the kind of head start your child requires to separate him from the common *Millionaires*-to-Be.

Vocabulary
- IPO
- NASDAQ
- REIT
- Ag
- Au
- S&P
- Dividend Yield
- NIKKEI
- Hang Seng
  (not hang ten)

Math Exercises
May be limited to:
- Addition • Multiplication

Recommended Reading
- *They're Lying! I Really Have a Billion!* by Donald Trump
- *Rockefeller Was a Pauper* by Bill Gates

Childhood Friends

It is extremely important not to allow your present and future asset to hang out with the hoi polloi. This includes your current neighborhood children, too, so move it! Cash in that 401(k), take out some major loans, and move to a neighborhood you can't afford. Go into debt, max out your credit cards, and live beyond your means. Way beyond.

Even at the earliest age, as he gazes out his nursery window and views the stately mansions and the Bentleys and Aston Martins whizzing by, your little one should come to believe that *everyone* lives this way. There should be no "less than rich" in his daily life. He should grow up believing that the Dollar Stores are a place where you buy money.

While the kids in your old neighborhood are learning T-ball and Pop Warner football, yours will be introduced to lacrosse, polo, tennis, and golf, the games that are ladylike or gentlemanly and only played by the "right people" (except for golf).

He must learn to compete with and excel in the "moneyed world." Above all else, do not allow him to have extended conversations with minimum-wage workers, K-Mart shoppers, or "trade" workers. The less he knows about the distasteful aspects of economic life the better.

The Teenage Years—*What's in Your Billionaire-to-Be's Room*

By the time your child reaches his teens, his room will give a good indication of where he's headed in life. Keep your eye out for any socialist tendencies (or if he shows even a fleeting interest in the Democratic Party). Here's what his room should look like if he's on the road to riches.

Decorating Tip
Repeating pattern of the daily New York Stock Exchange listings as wallpaper makes for a highly motivating decor while giving the room a bright and cheery feeling.

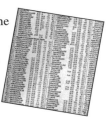

On his computer
- Last website visited: Ameritrade
- Last Google search: "Compound interest"
- Social networking site: www.superrich.org

In the trophy case
- 1st place, biggest grossing lemonade-stand sales, local Rotary Club contest, ten years running

On the nightstand
- *Fortune* • *The Economist*
- *The Wall Street Journal* (Caution! The appearance of *Money* indicates low aspirations)
- *The Big Book of Designer Logos*

On the wall
- Autographed poster of Bill Gates (boy) or Oprah Winfrey (girl)

The Guilt Factor

You're just about done, but there's still some work ahead. By this time, your little tyke has developed the right amount of *greed,* but it is your ongoing task to instill in him a complete lack of *guilt*. By the time he steps out into the world on his own, he should believe that if he has a billion or two and some people can't pay their rent—that's capitalism!

Guilt is a dangerous feeling. It can creep up when least expected, seeing as how there are so many really poor people on this planet. Even a small amount may cause your child to give unwarranted raises to his employees or needless money to charity, either of which could reduce his net assets and cause him to drop into the (gasp) centimillionaire level.

Therefore, this simple verbal exercise should be a part of your daily routine. Ask him to repeat out loud, "I earned it. It's mine!" whenever guilt pangs arise.

When he encounters people making a measly six- or seven-figure income, he should yell, "If you're poor, it's your own fault. Get a better job!"

Above all, he should be encouraged to smirk at lowly Mercedes or Lexus drivers, roll his eyes and sadly say, "They're trying so hard. Too bad they can't afford a Veyron like the rest of us."

Follow this routine religiously, and your child will be richly rewarded.

Raising Your Child to Become a
Nobel Prize Winner!

Degree of Difficulty
9.1

Whew! This is a tough one! How do you prepare your child to join the ranks of such luminaries as Yasser Arafat and Al Gore? And we're not talking your basic Nobel here; we're going to help you go for the big one: Peace! After all, who cares about economics anyway? It's like winning an Oscar for Best Best Boy.

So get ready to give peace a chance. This is not your average accomplishment, even for your little Superchild. Just have faith and follow our expert advice. We've got some dynamite suggestions.

Cost of Upbringing	Income Potential	Cost/Income Ratio
$$	$$$$$	**6.3** (1–10) Higher is better

Give Peace a Chance

Although not quite as exclusive as being a Pope (fifty in the last 500 years), nevertheless there have been only 777 individuals and twenty organizations that have been awarded the Nobel Prize. Therefore, your child will be in a very select club. The question is, which prize to go for?

We strongly recommend that you prepare your child for the Peace Prize as opposed to those of Physics, Chemistry, Medicine, Literature, or Economics. Why? A bit of history will help you understand.

Roger D. Kornberg was awarded the Nobel Prize in Chemistry, 2006, *"for his studies of the molecular basis of eukaryotic transcription."* Get that? Eukaryotic transcription.

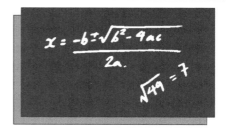

Elfriede Jelinek was awarded the Nobel Prize in Literature, 2004, *"for her musical flow of voices and counter-voices in novels and plays that, with extraordinary linguistic zeal, reveal the absurdity of society's clichés and their subjugating power."* Yeah, like your kid, even with our expert help, is going to write stuff like that!

In 1995, Robert Lucas was awarded the Nobel Prize in Economics *"for having developed and applied the hypothesis of rational expectations, and thereby having transformed macroeconomic analysis and deepened our understanding of economic policy.*" See what we mean?

The Nobel Prize in Physics, 2006, was awarded to John C. Mather and George F. Smoot *for their discovery of the blackbody form and anisotropy of the cosmic microwave background radiation.* Whew!

I hope by now you get our point. The above Nobel Prizes require some heavy thinking (see Home Tutoring at right). Winning the Peace Prize, on the other hand, is a piece of cake by comparison.

The beauty of the Peace Prize is that you can have another profession (like dictator or vice president) and then pick up the award. This means you could be a CEO of a major corporation pulling down a seven-figure salary and then claim the prize money as a "bonus." Meanwhile, the Literary Prize winner, for example, has to spend decades as a poor starving author, living hand-to-mouth, because his books are too serious to make the bestseller lists.

As John said, "Give peace a chance."

Home Tutoring

If you don't follow our advice, and you want to try for one of the other Nobel Prizes for your child, you're going to need a 4,000-book home library, a major investment in college tuition to the PhD level, and tons of tutors. This stuff is way too advanced for you to handle yourself.

Your child will then be faced with plodding away in her chosen field of endeavor for a few decades (economics for a few *decades*?) until the "brilliant idea" strikes. Or, since she can't make a ton of money being a physicist, you'll have to keep supporting her. We vote for Peace.

Boy? or Girl?

Don't worry. The Nobel committee is fair. No gender discrimination here. Girls have a chance, too.

Although Marie Curie was the first and only woman to be awarded the Nobel Prize in Physics (in 1903), she also holds the distinction of being the only woman, so far, to have been awarded the Nobel Prize for a second time when she received the 1911 Chemistry Prize.

The way things are going, Oprah should win Peace by 2011 and then Angelina a year or two later.

The Early Years

If you're going to give Peace a chance, you need to start preparing your child early, even though she won't reap the benefits of your parental skills for decades.

Your parenting chores for your little Peacekeeper-to-Be will revolve around her interaction with her friends, classmates, and siblings. At home she should be settling family squabbles by the time she's eight years old.

On the playground, school bullies provide much sought-after training in the important negotiating skills and "run-for-cover" tactics that will serve your child well later in life as she deals with insurgents and guerrillas. While other parents may try to handle the grade school bully problem by visiting the parents of the offender with a strong message and a baseball bat, we recommend that you allow the bullies to beat up your little one a few times until they tire of it and move on to other prey.

If your future Peacekeeper-to-Be can not learn to walk away from a fight, perhaps Bartender (see page 151) would be a better career choice.

Extracurricular Activities

Raising money selling candy bars is a popular do-good activity; however, we recommend that the proceeds not go to the school band, but for AIDS relief in Africa (resulting negotiations with band members will further improve your child's skills).

The United Nations

In today's world, most Americans don't pay attention to the United Nations. This will change by the time your Peacekeeper-to-Be 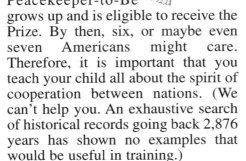 grows up and is eligible to receive the Prize. By then, six, or maybe even seven Americans might care. Therefore, it is important that you teach your child all about the spirit of cooperation between nations. (We can't help you. An exhaustive search of historical records going back 2,876 years has shown no examples that would be useful in training.)

Famous?

We hope you're in this for the cash because your little Peace Prize Winner-to-Be isn't going to gain a lot of fame except among people who actually read newspapers (other than tabloids), which eliminates 80 percent of the American public. Except for Al, Jimmy, and Yasser, who, of the following, is a household name for you?

- 2006 - Muhammad Yunus
- 2005 - Mohamed ElBaradei
- 2004 - Wangari Maathai
- 2003 - Shirin Ebadi
- 2002 - Jimmy Carter
- 2001 - Kofi Annan
- 2000 - Kim Dae-jung
- 1999 - Regis Philbin*
- 1998 - David Trimble
- 1996 - Carlos Filipe Ximenes Belo, José Ramos-Horta
- 1995 - Joseph Rotblat
- 1994 - Yasser Arafat
- 1992 - Rigoberta Menchú Tum
- 1991 - Aung San Suu Kyi

* Regis Philbin doesn't count. His name was added to see if you were paying attention.

Not much to do to prepare her room. Let her sleep. Let her dream. Let her cry (this is especially important, seeing what she's in for). Some soft music on the sound system, soft lights to soothe her. She's got a long way to go to achieve her (your) goal. She'll have enough pressure later in life. Give her some peace in her early years.

In the medicine cabinet
- *Lots of Band-Aids*

On the bookshelf
- *War and Peace*
- *The Strategy of Conflict*
- *Getting to Yes*
- *How to Negotiate Almost Anything*

On the wall
- Autographed poster of Mohandas Karamchand Gandhi. He never won, but you want your little one to dream.

Raising Your Child to Become a
Hall of Fame Athlete!

Degree of Difficulty
3.9

The beauty of raising the Hall of Fame Athlete is not in admiring his fluid grace as he charges across the field of competition. No, that's the end result. As much as you'll enjoy watching him perform, you'll enjoy raising him even more. Why? Because it's your *responsibility* to spoil the hell out of him from day one. As a star athlete, he'll be *rich* enough, you can be sure of that. But will he be *petulant* enough? *That's* up to you.

While other parents are feeling guilty about spoiling their kids, you'll be doing it with glee. With a vengeance! With a purpose! Sure, your little one will grow up to become a jerk, but—hey, he'll be in the *Hall*! To find out how to kick off his early training, read on . . .

<u>Cost of Upbringing</u>	<u>Income Potential</u>	<u>Cost/Income Ratio</u>
$$$	$$$$$$$$$$	**9.2** (1–10) Higher is better

52

Raising your child to become a Hall of Fame Athlete is, strangely enough, very similar to raising the Rock Star, as they will grow up to share many of the same "qualities."

Early on in life, you will need to spoil your child and instill in him an attitude of superiority and entitlement all out of proportion to his actual skills.

Athlete's medicine cabinet, circa 2026

You might think we will be recommending steriods or other chemical enhancements as your child's quickest and surest path to the Hall; however, this is not the case. Remember, it will be another sixteen to eighteen years before your little one is of contract-signing age, and times will surely be different then.

The future might not be any more ethical, but it will be different, and it is our goal to better prepare you and your child for times to come.

In the end, you will discover that it's really not that hard to qualify for the Hall. So follow our few simple rules, and get ready for the induction ceremony.

Home Tutoring

You may note that the Home Tutoring section for this chapter is much larger than those for other professions. This is because your kid will *not* do well in school if you bring him up right, so he will need more of your help at home.

By the time he graduates high school and signs his first big contract (if you have taught him correctly), he should have learned that it is not necessary for him to do any actual work or thinking to succeed. After all, he is going to be a professional athlete! We recommend that he major in home economics or sports sciences to keep things simple.

Use home tutoring time wisely by replaying uplifting sports films of Pontiac Game-Changing Moments (or news clips of mega-athletes signing mega contracts).

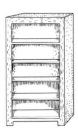

In the bookcase
- *Pouting for Dummies* by John McEnroe
- *Gladiators!* by Donald Trump
- *Team's Playbook* (Coach will send a copy home with him. You'll have to read it to him.)

Teach him to say:
- **The early years**
  "Yes, coach," "Sorry, coach," "I'll do better next time, coach."
- **The teen years**
  "Bug off, coach. I'm going to be a star and make a million times what you make."

Foreign language
No need for Latin or Greek, but he'll need to learn Xs and Os.

Get him ready for greatness (in his own mind, that is). And remember, success is not measured on the field of play but in the financial pages.

So keep him dreaming—not about record-breaking performances, but about record-breaking contracts. He'll be rich (at least for a few years).

Scattered about
Without the help of chemical performance enhancers, good old barbells will have to do.

One the mobile
• Shoes, shoes, shoes!

In the medicine cabinet
• Band-Aids, aspirin, and Tylenol

On the wall
No photos, just framed copies of A-Rod's blockbuster contract and the $100,000,000 LeBron James shoe contract, a stopwatch clock, and four "It's All About Me!" posters (one for each wall).

It's All About ME!

Show Me the Money!

It would seem reasonable to expect that if you raised your future Famer-to-Be as a football, basketball, baseball, or golf star, he will grow up to become rich and famous. But you purchased this book for our expert advice—and here it is: the sports that are hot now, in terms of big-money contracts (see top row below) will be out of vogue by the time your child is of bonus-signing age, and will be overtaken in popularity by other sports (see bottom row).

The NBA (National Badminton Association) is expected to be a juggernaut by the end of this decade. So prepare!

Football	**Basketball**	**Baseball**	**Golf**
Bowling	**Cricket**	**Badminton**	**Female Wrestling**

Shoe Me the Money

Okay, we've been kidding you all along in this chapter. None of what we said thus far is of any importance.

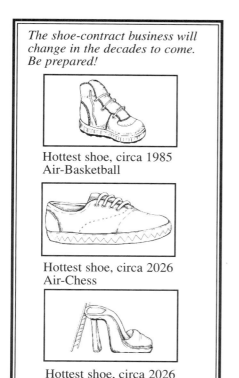

The shoe-contract business will change in the decades to come. Be prepared!

Hottest shoe, circa 1985
Air-Basketball

Hottest shoe, circa 2026
Air-Chess

Hottest shoe, circa 2026
Air–Female wrestling

Here is the real scoop: it's all about the shoes! If you don't get a shoe contract, you don't make it into the Hall of Fame. Heck, swimmers can't even make it into a Hall of Fame without a shoe contract.

Therefore, it is crucial for you as a parent to build a relationship with a shoe designer early. Face it, Michael Jordan was an average basketball player at best. He would have been nothing without a shoe contract and the Air Jordan.

The "Hall(s)"

Luckily, by the time your little one reaches contract-signing age, he will find it even easier to get into the "Hall" because there will be two of them.

Although there is currently a movement to call the second one the "Asterisk Hall," it is our belief that major league sports, looking for a more positive name, will probably go with "Regular Hall" and "Enhanced Hall."

We here at the Institute strongly advise you to plan in advance to qualify for the "Regular Hall." This is because by the time your little sports star grows up, he will be one of the few left not taking steroids, so he should be a shoo-in. Competition for the "Enhanced Hall" will be furious, since kids will be taking steroids before they start on solid foods.

The downside of his choice, of course, is that his shoe contract will be substantially smaller.

One Hall or two, the question remains, "How difficult is it, really, to qualify?" Not that hard, as the curve below will illustrate.

The Famous Albert Belle Curve

Discovered by the father of Albert Belle (who used it to get little Al into the Hall), the Belle Curve shows the distribution of talent, intelligence, and almost anything else throughout the general population. It says that 5 percent of any population will be inept, 5 percent will be stupendous, and the remaining 90 percent will be about average. And average is all your child will have to be to get into the Hall.

Baseball players with a lifetime batting average of .295 get in. If a person fails at something almost three out of four times, you would think he should be in a Hall of Shame. (Think of how fast you would fire your stock advisor if he or she had a track record like that.)

Quarterbacks get in if they complete about half of their passes. Half!

So in the end, your kid won't have to be in that upper 5 percent. About average will be good enough (but don't tell him that. Remember, he's a star!).

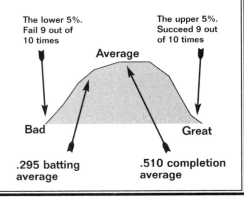

The lower 5%. Fail 9 out of 10 times

The upper 5%. Succeed 9 out of 10 times

Average

Bad

Great

.295 batting average

.510 completion average

Planning for Retirement

It's never too early.

It is not necessary for you to give your Hall of Famer-to-Be a good grounding in personal finances. Once he's been inducted into the Hall, he'll be able to make a good living well into his eighties without knowing anything about 401(k)s, IRAs, or pension plans.

When the really big bucks start rolling in, he'll have an agent (at least someone will get rich) and he'll start buying you and all his friends houses, cars, and bling. And then he'll be broke (retired) by forty. But not to worry, that's where the Hall comes in.

Your retired superstar will be able to make a good six-figure income signing autographs while doing the sports memorabilia show circuit. And, even though he made it through his entire career without a serious injury, he's sure to get carpel tunnel syndrome from signing 100 per day at $100 a crack.

He'll still be having fun, though, sitting in the lounge where his aging fans will be buying him drinks just for the pleasure of his company.

Just pray he doesn't notice that Rolls whizzing by outside. It will be his agent.

Raising Your Child to Become
Governor of California!

Degree of Difficulty
6.9

If you think we're California dreamin', you're wrong. It's easier than you might imagine for your child to qualify for—and win—this exciting job. The governatorship is considered by most to be a better job than President; after all, who needs all those international problems. Hollywood, Silicon Valley (and silicone valley), Napa Valley (and valley girls), Big Sur, and the Golden Gate Bridge—they'll all be yours, or at least your Superchild's.

So pack your bags, your suntan lotion, and your surfboard, and head for the Golden State; your child will need to be a resident. You'll be living there for the next thirty-five years. It's one of the perks of raising the future Governor of California!

Cost of Upbringing	Income Potential	Cost/Income Ratio
$$$$	$$$$$$	**6.8** (1–10) Higher is better

The Primaries

Before you make your decision, pack your surfboard and your tie-dyed T-shirts, and move to the Golden State, there are some things you should know. This is not your average Governorship your child is going to be seeking. The basic requirement is to be a little "off center." And we don't mean that in a political sense. In a state whose polititans have included George Murphy, Pat Brown, Ronald Reagan, John Wayne, and the Governator, you might think that the only qualifications would be a goofy, dancing, muscular actor. And you wouldn't be far from the truth. But this is the first decade of the twenty-first century. By the time your little one is of vote-getting age, the definition of "weird" is going to change and you must prepare him for this eventuality. But more on that later.

For the time being, you can comfort yourself with the knowledge that running for office in this state puts your child in excellent company. The 2003 California recall election resulted in voters replacing incumbent

Democratic Governor Gray Davis with Republican Arnold ("I'll be back") Schwarzenegger. And running right alongside the big boys was porn star Mary Carey as an Independent candidate, *placing tenth in a field of 135 candidates*. She ran on a ten-point platform, promising, among other things, to tax breast implants and make lap dances tax deductible.

Of course, this only points out the fact that *anybody* can run (and, as recent history has shown, you don't even have to be able to speak English). Yes, anybody can *run,* but the objective is to get your kid into the winner's circle.

Understanding the Constituency

Contrary to popular belief, California is full of relatively normal people. The state is broken down into roughly three zones: The first, including all people within one mile of the ocean, is the "Weird Zone," where people whom the rest of the country thinks of as "true Californians" reside.

The second zone, slightly farther inland, is populated by people almost as weird as those in the Weird Zone,

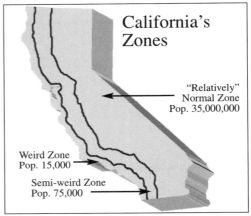

California's Zones

"Relatively" Normal Zone
Pop. 35,000,000

Weird Zone
Pop. 15,000

Semi-weird Zone
Pop. 75,000

but they can't afford to live there.

The third zone is where 99 percent of the population lives, and they are "relatively" normal. Not as normal as, say, the people of Boise, Idaho, or Graceland or Transylvania, but, nevertheless, pretty normal.

So, as you can plainly see now that we have pointed this out, if your little Governor-to-Be wants to prevail in the election, he should be paying attention to the population in Zone . . . *wrong!*

You were going to answer "the zone with all the people," weren't you?

The reason your answer is incorrect lies in understanding the mentality of "relatively" normal Californians. You see, they moved to the state because they dreamed of being wonderfully weird—bought into the California Dream—but lost their way or ran out of gas before they got to the coast. Nevertheless, they still believe deep in their hearts that they are just like the "coastals," and will follow their lead. So, we're back to the weird ones you will have to impress if you want to win.

The Alien Question

As we mentioned earlier, the Governators of the great state of California are getting stranger and stranger. So your child has his work cut out for him. It's possibly thirty years before his run for the statehouse. What will be defined as "strange" by then?

Here's the scoop. By 2038, there will be an illegal alien on the ticket opposing your little one. But here's the real scoop: it will be a *real* illegal alien, not some landscape contractor who worked his way up the party heirachy. The Earth is sure to have "visitors" by then. And would you like to hazard a guess as to which state they will visit first?

So get busy. Your child could very well be the last earthling to rule California before an alien takes office (although some of Schwarzenegger's detractors would argue that fact). Don't miss your chance. You can be sure that once Californians elect their first alien, they'll never look back.

The Importance of the Diet

Here's some good news: you're going to save a lot on food while raising your little tyke. As Caifornians progress (?) from being 60 percent carnivorious, 30 percent vegetarian, and 10 percent vegan, to 80 percent vegetarian, and 20 percent

Governator 2035?

65

vegan, there will be a movement to *stop eating entirely* by the time your child is ready to win votes. Californians will be getting their sustenance from simply breathing their air, which will, by this time, be pure and free of any "stuff." Californians will have ended obesity and saved valuable resources as well. (Farmworkers will not complain because they will all be legal by this time and will have moved on to jobs in Hollywood.)

We recommend that you start your little one off on a strictly vegan diet and switch to total food abstinence by the time he reaches his teens.

Oh, and by the way, don't worry about the housing prices in Zone 1. Since you won't have to move just yet, buy a nice piece of property now in Zone 3 and wait a bit. It won't be your fault, but you'll be living on the ocean by the time you arrive.

Home Tutoring

There's not a lot for you to do when your little Governor-to-Be is young. Painting his room green is so obvious we hesitate to mention it. But just so he doesn't think it's that easy to be green, place a stuffed Kermit the Frog in his toy box. Teach him to ride a bike (there'll be no cars in the state by then). Make sure he buffs up (you'll understand when you see who his opponent will be). Finally, make sure he watches *Teletubbies* in his spare time. If he's going to be weird, this is a good place to start.

Fun, Educational Activity

You can be sure that the green movement will still be thriving in California when your child runs for office. Here's a fun activity that not only builds physical strength, but also increases your little one's emotional bond with our friends, the trees.

Step 1. Approach tree slowly so as not to frighten it.

Step 2. Wrap arms around tree. Hug gently. Release. Repeat.

Step 3. Step back. Smile at tree. Say, "Nice tree."

Creating Your Platform

Take your time; originality counts. Here is a quick synopsis of the most successful platforms proposed by Governors-to-Be in the past few decades so you can avoid proposing the same old issues.

- Tax breast implants (been there)
- Legalize pot (done that)
- Support free speech (again?)
- Oppose war (again?)
- Eject aliens (2002)
- Welcome aliens (2042)

- Protect transsexuals and cross-dressers in hiring and employment practices (of course)

Instead, we recommend that you build your campaign around animal rights. By the time your child runs for office, California will have voted to grant animals citizenship. Have him show his support for animal rights and be the first to choose an animal as a running mate.

We recommend a Lab.

Understanding Propositions

If your little Governor-to-Be is going to be successful as ruler of the people, it will be necessary for him to understand that strange California affection: the Proposition. (No, not the Hollywood Boulevard kind of proposition, the political one.)

A proposition is basically a way Californians have figured out to circumvent whoever is in power and vote on what they want to. If the Governator wants a vote on the fiscal stability of the state, and the populace want to vote on whether to tax Twinkies, Twinkies get on the ballot. Interestingly, this is very clever. This way, Californians don't feel they have to elect anyone smart or someone who has their best interests in mind, which can only work to your child's advantage if he is not very smart.

Conclusion
"I'll be back"

You're probably thinking to yourself, "If only I knew who my child's opponent will be thirty years from now. It would make things much easier."

Don't despair. As you would expect, we have the answer for you. This *is* California we're talking about, remember, and the sequel is king.

He said he'd be back, and he will be. Therefore, we recommend you check to see whether Sarah Conner is still around; you're going to need some help.

READER/CUSTOMER CARE SURVEY

HEMG

We care about your opinions! Please take a moment to fill out our online Reader Survey at **http://survey.hcibooks.com**. As a **"THANK YOU"** you will receive a **VALUABLE INSTANT COUPON** towards future book purchases as well as a **SPECIAL GIFT** available only online! Or, you may mail this card back to us.

First Name _____ MI. _____ Last Name _____

Address _____ Zip _____ City _____

State _____ Email _____

1. Gender
☐ Female   ☐ Male

2. Age
☐ 8 or younger
☐ 9-12   ☐ 13-16
☐ 17-20   ☐ 21-30
☐ 31+

3. Did you receive this book as a gift?
☐ Yes   ☐ No

4. Annual Household Income
☐ under $25,000
☐ $25,000 - $34,999
☐ $35,000 - $49,999
☐ $50,000 - $74,999
☐ over $75,000

5. What are the ages of the children living in your house?
☐ 0 - 14   ☐ 15+

6. Marital Status
☐ Single
☐ Married
☐ Divorced
☐ Widowed

Comments _____
_____
_____
_____
_____

BUSINESS REPLY MAIL

FIRST-CLASS MAIL PERMIT NO 45 DEERFIELD BEACH, FL

POSTAGE WILL BE PAID BY ADDRESSEE

Health Communications, Inc.
3201 SW 15th Street
Deerfield Beach FL 33442-9875

Raising Your Child to Become a
Celebrity Chef!

**Degree of Difficulty
5.0**

Long hours in a sweltering kitchen? Flipping burgers at some fast-food joint? Not *your* child. She'll be a Food Network star, doing the book-signing circuit, and rearranging little pieces of her creations on pretty plates for rock stars and heads of state. And when your Celebrity Chef comes home to visit, you won't have to cook!

Preparing your child for this profession has plenty of other perks for you, too. While the rest of the neighborhood is eating microwavable pizzas, your teenager will be throwing together meals like Duck Cordon Bleu with Green Peppercorn Sauce. And the parental training isn't difficult—we've got the right recipe—just follow our expert advice and, as a bonus, you'll get all the leftovers.

Cost of Upbringing	Income Potential	Cost/Income Ratio
$$$$	$$$$$$$	**9.2** (1–10) Higher is better

70

The Early Years

It would seem there would be a simple recipe for raising a Celebrity Chef: toss together a few good cookbooks, add some home ec courses at school, then turn the little one loose in the kitchen. Oh, that it were so easy!

Perhaps that was enough in the good old days when rock stars were just musicians and chefs were just cooks, but in today's celebrity-obsessed world, it's not enough. Her training had better start at birth and had better be right!

A little history may be in order. For generations it was only the French (and sometimes the Italians) who produced the world's great chefs (and the first Celebrity Chefs). This was because we were stifling our children with that dreaded phrase, "Don't play with your food!" The French, on the other hand, were yelling, "Vous dhv zee votre strained peas!" which translates (loosely) to "Go ahead, throw your strained peas at me, what do I care? Someday you will be zee Celebrity Chef." The Italians just made theatrical hand gestures to their kids, but the message was the same.

So, Rule #1: Let her play with her food. After all, if things go right, she'll be earning big money doing exactly the same thing in just a few years.

When you whisk your precious Celebrity Chef-to-Be home from the hospital, make sure her nursery is on the cutting edge. Set the VCR to play endless loops of the Food Network, and proceed with the following:

In the cradle
- *Food & Wine* (Lifetime subscription)
- Her first toque
- Famous Chefs of the World trading cards

On the bookshelf
- Anthony Bourdain's *Kitchen Confidential;* George Orwell's *Down and Out in Paris and London;* George LeBorts's *Trotter's: Of Pigs and Charlies*

Trotter's
Of Pigs
and
Charlies

Charlie

On the wall
- Chef of the Year award from the James Beard Foundation, with her name inserted. Postdated to 2025

Chef of
the Year
2025

In the toy box
- Play stove
- Fisher Price Food Processor
- 24-piece famous cookware set
- Professional set of Wusthof knives

On the wall
- Autographed photo of Julia Childs (girls)
- Autographed photo of Julia Childs (boys)

Naming Your Child

You must be prepared for your boy's schoolmates to call him a wuss. Your girl will be demeaningly referred to as little homemaker-to-be. But this is a small price to pay for the fame and fortune that awaits. Actually, a bigger problem is getting her through the early knife-playing years.

She can always take a "stage name" later in life. If you want to start her off right, however, here are our suggestions:

Recommended Celebrity Chef-to-Be Names:

- Julia (girl)
- Jullienne (boy)
- Zagat
- Pierre
- Emiril
- Michelle (girl)
- Michelin (boy)

Names Not Recommended

- Thumbs

Home Tutoring

Most schools don't teach French in the first grade, and since your little one will already have a sizable cookbook collection by that time, a bit of French at home is necessary. Tip: start with the French pronoun "zee."

Vocabulary
- Sauté
- Zee whisk
- Zee bain-marie
- Foie gras
- Zee pot
- Zee pan
- Zee spoon

Very little Italian is necessary. The following vocabulary should take your little tyke through culinary school and beyond:
- Pasta
- Red Sauce

Recommended Reading
Larousse Gastronomique by Prosper Montagne

The Fungus Among Us: 10,000 Mushroom Creations by George LeBorts

The current restaurant craze that sanctifies chefs and turns their kitchens into shrines has also turned their headwear into the next hip and trendy thing. Wear one yourself to let everyone know what fame is in store for your little one, and follow our advice below to the letter.

The Proper Toque

Toque (which means "stupid-looking paper hat" in French) is thought to have originated in China and to be the first item created after the invention of paper. Their invention of the escargot soon followed.

Today, fast-food chefs still wear the paper variety, but all *Celebrity* Chefs wear toques made of 40,000-count Egyptian cotton.

Get your kid a proper cotton toque immediately, even though she will be teased relentlessly in culinary school for "toquing-up." But she'll get the last laugh when she's the first one with a million-dollar cookbook contract.

Wearing It Correctly

True Celebrity Chefs let the top droop casually, as if to say, "Look, my touque is drooping casually!"

Incorrect

Incorrect

Correct

<u>How to Chop an Onion</u>

Teaching Your Celebrity Chef-to-Be Proper Knife Use:

This will certainly be taught in culinary school, but giving your child a head start is the kind of parenting that guarantees success. For safety reasons, we recommend waiting until your child is at least four before you begin this training.

1. Using a very sharp knife, cut off the end of the onion.

2. Turn onion so it rests on the newly cut flat surface.

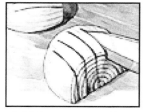

3. Make some cuts this way. It's fun!

4. Now cut it this way. Whew! It's a lot of work to cut one little onion, yes?

5a. Congratulations! If you followed our instructions, you'll have a perfectly chopped onion. High five!

5b. Whooops! Go back to step 1 and carefully review our instructions. High four!

Road Trips!

It is critical that you assist your little Celebrity Chef-to-Be as early as possible in the development of her taste buds. The best way to accomplish this is to see that she samples excellent, as well as disgusting, food.

Stop at fast-food restaurants whenever you are out and about. By the time she is four years old, she should be able to tell the difference between a Whopper, a Slider, and a Big Mac and make her determination as to which is best. As she grows older and you begin weaning her from this fare, you will start taking her to a wide variety of high-quality "sit-down" restaurants, such as Houlihans, Fridays, and Chilis. She will probably long for that Slider, but keep her on the straight and narrow for a week or two. By that time, she will have tired of the extensive menus offered by the above establishments and you can move on to that Holy Grail: White Tablecloth Restaurants, where you will spend much of your time and most of your retirement savings keeping your little one up on the latest culinary trends and innovations.

The French Connection

Face it. It's a fact of life. You're going to have to send your kid to France. She may become a *chef* without some French training, but never a *Celebrity* Chef. *Mais non!*

But here's the catch. Here's the critical part that most parents—at least those who have not had the foresight to purchase this book—miss:

> *One does not go to Paris*
> *for the culinary training.*
> *One goes to learn the*
> *arrogance and pomposity*
> *that separates the mere chef*
> *from the true Celebrity Chef.*

Your child is never going to make it big on the Food Network without a serious attitude, and there's no better place than Paris to pick one up. Upon returning, she will be able to scream at her minions, *"You fool! Can't you even chop zee onion properly?"* Whereas the unfortunate chef who never trained in France would probably say "the" onion, and nobody would pick up her pilot for production.

Another reason your child needs to acquire such an attitude is because of the big letdown she will experience when she returns from France. After spending years learning to create culinary masterpieces, she'll discover what she should have known all along: Americans prefer nachos. But instead of screaming "You stupid fool!" at a customer, she can let her attitude say it for her.

And finally, when she's had enough, she can sell out and open a restaurant in Las Vegas.

Editor's Note

If at any time during your child's formative years she shows any tendencies toward creating fusion cuisine, perhaps she would be better suited to be a nuclear scientist.

The Hollywood Connection

In addition to Paris, your child will have to make the trek to Hollywood because even more important than knowing how to cook will be her ability to look good on TV. While she's in town, she should take some acting lessons, sign up an agent, and start shmoozing some celebrities who will one day finance her expensive restaurant venture (and certainly lose every cent of their investment).

Sure, these trips are going to cost you. But, hey, that's what doting parents are for! And think of the great food you'll get at her restaurant! Just don't forget to make reservations!

Typical Time Line

How is your little Celebrity Chef-to-Be doing? Is she on track to becoming one of the all-time greats? It's important to check her progress against those who have preceded her. Here's how to tell whether your tyke is measuring up.

- Trains at restaurant Le Sans Souci, Paris (age 12)
- Creates first "signature dish" (age 13)
- Authors her first cookbook (age 14)
- Authors her first best-selling cookbook (age 16)
- First TV appearance (age 17)
- Her own TV show (age 18)
- Opens first restaurant (age 21)
- Gets first Michelin star (same year)
- "Sells out" and opens restaurant in Las Vegas. Says "That's where the gourmets are." (age 22)

Raising Your Child to Become a
Chess Master!

Degree of Difficulty
7.0

One advantage of raising your child to become a Chess Master (as opposed to Pope, for example) is that you won't have to wait years and years for him to become a success. By the time he's eight, you should be basking in his limelight. This means there is no long-term commitment on your part, and since there's not a lot of expensive equipment to buy, you're pretty much home free on this one.

The money won't be too bad, either. By the time your child is ready, the championship purses will have grown dramatically as our next generation begins to admire brains over brawn. Of course, if money was your main consideration, you would be reading the Billionaire chapter instead of this one.

On the downside, you'll have to live with the fact that all your friends will think your kid is smarter than you (and, of course, he will be).

Cost of Upbringing	Income Potential	Cost/Income Ratio
$$$	$$$$$$$	8.1 (1–10) Higher is better

Your First Move

First, the bad news: you're going to have to learn about the Nimzo-Larsen Attack, the Budapest Gambit, and the Benoni Defense so you can point your kid in the right direction. Now the good news: you won't have to actually *understand* any of this chess gobbledygook; just pronouncing it will be enough. After he's viewed repeats of the videos of these strategies from his crib, he'll be spouting theories more complex than these before he's five.

Of course, learning the pronunciation for the above mentioned strategies is difficult enough, even for a parent as dedicated as you are. Your first thought might be to invest in a full-blown Russian-language course, but we recommend simply hiring a Russian au pair.

And all this is just for the early years. As you will learn later, to increase his odds your little one will soon be *moving* to Russia. At least Communism is dead, you'll be able to get a decent job (or get Russian citizenship for the little tyke), and you'll get an annual government stipend.

Other than this, your task is relatively simple . . .

The Early Years—Preparing Your Chess Master-to-Be's Room

One complaint we have received from parents who have raised Superchild Chess Masters in the past has been the constant headaches and eyestrain caused by all the black-and-white squares in their children's rooms. Trust us, it won't bother your kid. He'll be too entranced by the endless loops shown on the TV (see below).

Knight Rocking Horse

Playhouse
• Play castle in the shape of a rook

On the walls
• Unique black-and-white squares design for wallpaper

In the crib
• Unique black-and-white squares design fabric for baby's blanket/pj's, etc.

On the floor
• Unique black-and-white squares design for floor tiles

On the bedside table
• Knight light
• *Lasker's Manual of Chess* by Emanuel Lasker

On the wall
• Framed autographed photo of Bobby Fisher

On TV
• Endless DVDs of the Dutch Defense and the Iljin-Zhenevsky Variation

Educational Games to Play with Your Child

People may think chess is 100 percent mental, but past champions have shown us the value of physical conditioning.

The two following activities are so much fun you can tell your child they are just games when, in reality, they are serious strength and reflex-building exercises that will help prepare him for stardom!

Whack-a-Timer

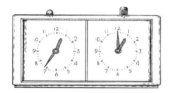

Based on the famous Whack-a-Mole arcade game, this fun game will keep your Chess Master-to-Be enthralled for hours. You whack, the timer resets, he whacks, the timer resets. It's fun. It's educational!

This game will build up his reflexes so he can advance to the Hand-to-Pawn game (at right).

Hand-to-Pawn Coordination

This exercise is a lot of fun and it's not much more difficult than teaching a dog to fetch. Place pawn on table in front of your infant, then whisk it away before he can react. This will make him cry, but he will learn quickly. By the time he's four, he'll be stealing pawns from every kid in the neighborhood. And making *them* cry.

Overcoming the Nerd Factor

Don't worry about your kid growing up with people laughing at him for being a nerd or a chess geek. Forget about your own childhood when bullies beat up on any kid with a brain. The public is already growing tired of petulant, steroid-infused, underachieving, misogynistic professional athletes. By the time your kid is old enough to play in professional championship chess matches (four years from now), we will have moved on to worshipping the more cerebral  sporting events, such as chess and beach volleyball. Chess masters will be the Tom Bradys of tomorrow!

It is important that you be the type of parent who can see beyond the obvious (quarterback = $$$$$), and be willing to place your bet that in the near future, we will be watching reality chess matches with the same enthusiasm we watch *The Next Top Supermodel* today.

Move to Russia?

For the past eight *decades*, the World Championship has been held by Russia/USSR for, well, for most of the time. Our advice? Get a visa (it must be in the water).

Alex Alekhine, **Russia/France**
1927–1935, 1937–1945
Max Euwe, Netherlands
1935-1937
Mikhail Botvinnik, **USSR**
1948–1957, 1958–1960,
1961–1963
Vasily Smyslov, **USSR**
1957–1958
Mikhail Tal, **USSR**
1960–1961
Tigran Petrosian, **USSR**
1963–1969
Boris Spassky, **USSR**
1969–1972
Robert Fischer, USA
1972–1975
Anatoly Karpov, **USSR**
1975–1985
Garry Kasparov, **USSR**
1985–2000
Vladimir Kramnik, **Russia**
2000–2006

Extracurricular Activities

The easiest part of being the parent of

a Chess Master-to-Be will be your task of finding extracurricular activities for him to participate in. This is because there will be none.

Chess, chess, chess. And more chess. Morning, noon, and night. Extracurricular activities are for people who have lives. And this will certainly not be the case with your fortunate child. He will not get the mixed signals received by other children ("Why is studying good now, and playing baseball good at another time? Why can't I play baseball all the time if it's good?")

It's your job to protect your little Master-to-Be from traumatizing thoughts and questions such as these. No reading (except chess manuals), no movies (except *The Bobby Fischer Story)*, no TV, no camping, no fishing, no Boy or Girl Scouts. And, please, no dating!

Becoming Chess Champion is all about focus. It is your job to see that your child focuses on focusing. Can we put this any more in focus?

Danger Signals

One easy way to tell if you are succeeding in your parental duties is to constantly observe your child, looking for bright eyes and a healthy, ruddy complexion.

Healthy, eight-year-old Chess Master-to-Be

Danger signals such as these should not be ignored. More board time is usually a good remedy. You will know you are back on track when you observe his eye sockets again begin to recede.

The Final Gambit

This rather simple gambit (the famous Russo-Hungarian Defense, Ilich-Propenski Variation, with mayo on the side) should be mastered before he proceeds to more complex strategies—around the age of six.

Raising Your Child to Become a
Celebutant!

Degree of Difficulty
0.8

Come on . . . admit it. Here's the "profession" you've really been flipping through this book for. As you devour the tabloids every day, you find yourself saying, "How *do* they do it? They don't do a lick of work—just party day and night. That's the kind of 'job' I'd like."

Well, devoted parent, it may be too late for you, but don't despair. Follow our simple instructions, and you'll discover it's a no-brainer (just like the result). And now that everyone's started calling them "Celebutants" instead of bimbos, you won't even be embarrassed to say to the world, "That's my girl!"

Cost of Upbringing	Income Potential	Cost/Income Ratio
$	$$$$$	8.0 (1–10) Higher is better

You'll be able to laugh at your friends who worry endlessly that their children might get caught up in drugs, underage drinking, nightclub brawling, and adolescent sex. Your only worry will be that your child *isn't* partaking of these fame-building, fun activities.

After all, how will your little one make the tabloids without a little spice in her life?

Her clothing budget will pose a problem, as she will need everything fashionable. Lots of it. And when it's HOT—not two weeks later. It is during this period that you will explain that "shopping" does *not* involve a grocery cart. As the dutiful parent, you will need to learn to pay for your purchases with a subtle "Send me the bill," or at least have the credit card transaction take place out of sight of your Celebutant-to-Be. She must *never* discover that clothes and accessories are actually paid for.

And get ready to convert your

master bedroom into her walk-in closet. You and your spouse will sleep in the guest bedroom to make room for Armani, et al. You'll get your space back when she turns sixteen and is ready to move out and party without parental supervision (not that you've been giving her any, anyway, if you've been doing your job).

Flash me!
Here's a Fun, Educational Game to Play

Flash cards are a proven educational tool. Make flashing a game, and she'll love to practice with you. Soon she'll be able to recognize all the important designer logos in a millisecond (and spot those nasty counterfeits, too).

While other children are getting flashed with multiplication tables and Latin verbs, yours will be learning the important stuff!

And remember, it's important she get the pronunciation right: Ermenegildo Zegna is Ere-milli-zill-gee-and-goo-do, and that's a hard V in Bvlgari (Bull-VEE-gary).

The Early Years—Preparing Your Celebutant-to-Be's Room

Of course you'll reserve a limo to get your little princess home from the hospital. She can never start too early. And her room will be ready with full-length mirrors and spot-lights! (She will want to start primping early.) Scatter issues of *People* about, and the tabloids. No need to get her a subscription; she'll soon be on the "comp" list.

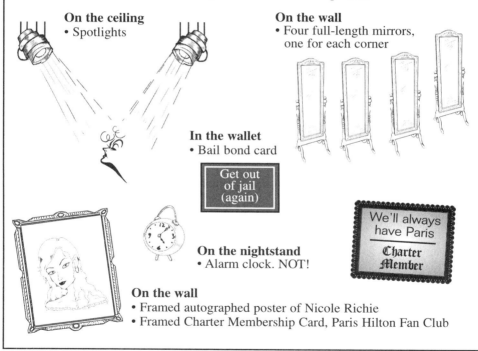

On the ceiling
• Spotlights

On the wall
• Four full-length mirrors, one for each corner

In the wallet
• Bail bond card

Get out of jail (again)

On the nightstand
• Alarm clock. NOT!

We'll always have Paris

Charter Member

On the wall
• Framed autographed poster of Nicole Richie
• Framed Charter Membership Card, Paris Hilton Fan Club

Celebutant Technology

Strange as it may seem, your little Celebutant-to-Be will have no need for a computer by the time she reaches "maturity." Her Fab 500 list, 18,000 iTunes, and Social Networking Page will all be easily accessible on her iPhone. What else is there? Oh, yeah, her bail bondsman's number.

Put the money you saved by not buying that new, sleek Mac Powerbook toward that new, hot clutch of the week. She'll get much more use out of it anyway.

Social Networking Page

HOME BROWSE SEARCH INVITE MAIL BLOGS FAVORITES GROUPS

Tiffini

Tiffini is in your extended network

"That's hot, bitch!"

Female
26 years old

Los Angeles

About me:
"I'm hot!"
Who I'd like to meet:
"Anyone as hot as me!"
Tiffini's friends
Tiffini has a gazillion friends

Tiffini's Interests

| GENERAL | Clubbing Shopping |
| BOOKS | What? |

Tiffini's Friends' Comments

Loved your sex tape!

✣ Click here to see my sex tape

Teaching the Correct Paparazzi Pose

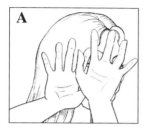

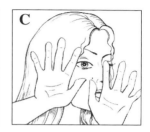

It's critical that you teach your little Celebutant-to-Be the proper "Hands in front of face" pose for those sudden, unexpected paparazzi moments. Too much face coverage (A) and what's the point? Nobody will recognize her. Not enough face coverage (B) and it looks fake, as in, "Please put my picture in the paper!" The perfect pose is (C): "Oh, dear me, I'm trying to hide, but you can still see my fabulous new eye job!"

I'm Sorry, So Sorry . . .

Preparing your child for her inevitable (and many) apologies will be an important part of your parenting duties. Remember, these will not be private-affair apologies between you and her or between her and her boy toy of the week. No, these must be public, and you can be sure there will be "press" and microphones aplenty, so it's important that her statements have a ring of truth to them.

Please provide your Celebutant-to Be with a pack of Stock Apology forms (shown below right). She will undoubtedly be under stress during times such as these and the "check the box" simplicity of these useful forms will come in handy. Insist that she practice in advance in front of family and friends until she sounds contrite.

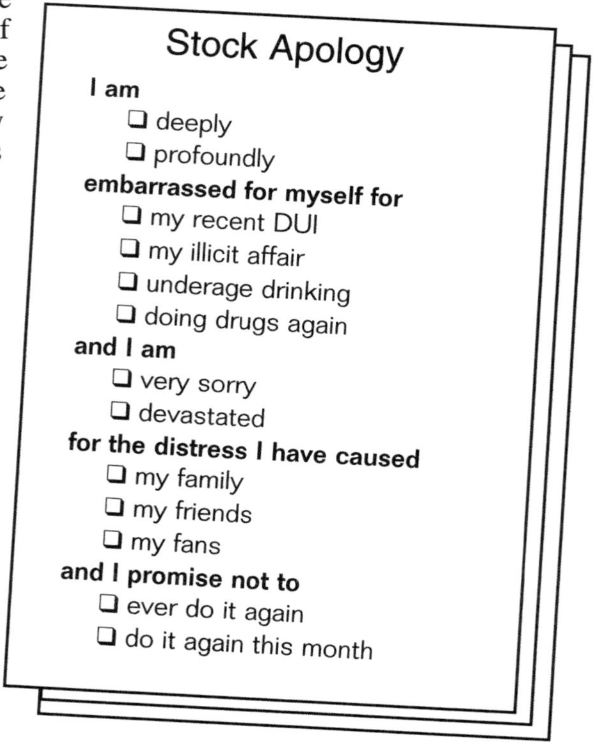

Stock Apology

I am
- ❏ deeply
- ❏ profoundly

embarrassed for myself for
- ❏ my recent DUI
- ❏ my illicit affair
- ❏ underage drinking
- ❏ doing drugs again

and I am
- ❏ very sorry
- ❏ devastated

for the distress I have caused
- ❏ my family
- ❏ my friends
- ❏ my fans

and I promise not to
- ❏ ever do it again
- ❏ do it again this month

Raising Your Child to Become a
TV News Anchor!

Degree of Difficulty
1.3

"*Wow!* I can't believe you're a real TV News Anchor!" That's the kind of worshipping comment your kid will receive day in and day out because, believe me, *everybody* will be impressed!

Of all the Superchild professions discussed in this book, creating the TV News Anchor is one of the easiest for the parent. Sure, there's some work involved. Not only will you have to make sure that your child can actually read, but he'll also have to have a powerful command of makeup techniques as well. Your orthodontist bills will be substantial, too, since perfect teeth and a great smile are a must. But all in all, you're in for a relatively leisurely twenty-five years of parenting. And there's fame and fortune awaiting your child (unless the Internet causes TV news to become extinct by the time your child is ready to go on the air!).

Cost of Upbringing	Income Potential	Cost/Income Ratio
$$	$$$$$	**5.8** (1–10) Higher is better

Tips for the Early Years

For you parents out there who don't want to put too much effort into raising a Superchild, here's a profession for your little tyke that doesn't require a lot of intensive parenting. It pays very well and offers a reasonable amount of fame (go figure!), so the effort-reward ratio is excellent.

And if your child shares your lack of a strong work ethic, he will thank you for choosing this profession for him. Because once he ascends to the Anchor's chair, he's not looking at a whole lot of overtime or even hard work in general.

Most parents who desire to raise their own real live News Anchor make the mistake of placing too much emphasis on academics. Please be cautioned that it is *not* necessary. Too much success in academics may cause your child to pursue a more demanding profession. Allow him to slack off a bit in his studies and develop other important skills, such as proper eye contact and sitting with proper posture.

And force him to focus on perfecting that all-important paper shuffling technique! This cannot be emphasized enough. He may rebel against tough drills such as this, but the future rewards will be worth it.

The Early Years—Preparing Your TV News Anchor-to-Be's Room

Before your Anchor-to-Be arrives home from the hospital, his room must be prepared properly. The home model TelePrompTer is a must. Before those tiny eyes focus on you, they should be able to follow the scrolling text with ease. Replace all incandescent bulbs (including night-light) with 150-watt spotlights. And remember, when you ever so slightly dim the spots to say "good night," as Uncle Walter gazes down upon your sleepy tyke, say softly you hope you'll see him tomorrow. Same time, same station.

In the cradle
- Microphone-shaped rattle
- First set of braces
- Jammies with anchor logo

Within sight of the cradle
TelePrompTer loaded with proper words and phrases, so that his first full sentence should be "We interrupt our regularly scheduled programming . . ."

In the toy box
- *The Place to Be* by Roger Mudd
- Makeup kit
- Special "Anchor Set" of blocks. Contains only important letters. Lots of Ns but no X (so he can't spell FOX by mistake).

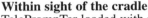

On the wall
- Framed autographed photo of Walter Cronkite

The All-Important Sign-Off

It's never too early to create one

Ever since Edward R. Murrow made "Good night and good luck" his famous, signature sign-off, it's been de rigueur for anchormen and anchorwomen to have their own unique, clever, pithy, and heartwarming close to their newscasts.

Walter Cronkite's "And that's the way it is" is another classic, and Katie Couric once held a contest to create hers because she couldn't think of one herself.

Of course, nothing but the most clever sign-off will do for your little Anchorperson. Without a great one, he won't be loved.

Starting about the age of three or four months, you must start his training. Every night after singing a lullaby, you will be sending a subliminal message to your young one when you utter one of the classic sign-offs. He'll be subconsciously learning what sounds *just right* at the end of the day.

No more "sweet dreams." Sign off instead.

Note: If he likes the choice of profession you've trained him for, perhaps his sign-off will be: *"Thanks to my parents, I'm famous and you're not!"*

Home Tutoring

Getting an early start on the specific vocabulary and speech patterns necessary to become a TV News Anchor is crucial. But this will be a fun time for you because, in addition to key words and phrases, you will be teaching your child *happy talk*!

Teach him the complicated phrases below and—then comes the hard part—how to pronounce them the weird way Anchors have to talk. This may take months of concentrated effort on his part.

Key Phrases:
"And when we come back . . ."
"And now back to you."
"In an exclusive report . . ."

Proper Emphasis:
"And when we come ***back*** . . ."
"And **now** . . . back to you."
"In an *e x c l u s i v e* report . . ."

His room should be neat and organized, not cluttered with extensive reading material and reference books (who needs all that stuff, anyway? Everything appears magically on the TelePrompTer). The number of mirrors should have increased exponentially—and the camcorder finally appears. If you hear voices when you know he's alone, don't worry. He's either practicing his happy-talk chortle or his Emmy Award acceptance speech.

On the hard drive
• Practice clips: First interview at age six, with Daddy and Mommy; paper-shuffling drills; happy-talk practice with friends

Camcorder
Always on (and so is he). He'll love to rewind and play back his every move and be amazed at how great he looks on camera

Required furnishings
Mirrors, mirrors on the wall . . .

On the wall
• Autographed poster of Geraldo Rivera made into dartboard

In the trophy case
• 42nd place: National Debating Society (your Anchor-to-Be won't be a standout, but who needs debating skills?

Teaching Professional Paper Shuffling 101

As a full-fledged News Anchor, your little one will be required to shuffle papers in a professional manner. Obviously, the earlier he masters this difficult activity the more professional he will look on camera. It will also be your job to convince him that the viewing audience is actually fooled by this.

Here's a fun activity you can do with your child while increasing the amount of quality time you spend together (we told you that raising an Anchor was not rocket science). Follow these simple instructions. It's not as difficult as it looks. *For a complete how-to demonstration, see YouTube.com/dotheanchorshuffle.*

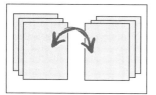

Step 1. Pick up papers from pile 1 and place on pile 2.

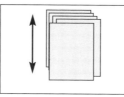

Step 2. Pick up combined piles and tap on desk a few times until neat.

Step 3. Replace pile on desk in front of you. Smile at camera.

Q & A

Asking the Proper Soft Questions

Before your child leaves high school, you should begin to focus your efforts on teaching the art of asking the perfect "soft question." This will be difficult at the beginning because he is used to asking hard questions, like "Can I smoke dope?" Since the answer to this requires some thought, this would qualify as an improper "hard question." "Nice day, isn't it?" is more along the lines of what you're looking for.

Soft questions are important because Anchors *do* like to talk. And the problem is that no one will want to talk to them if they persist in asking questions that make a person uncomfortable. Or require others to actually think.

This may sound like an easy skill to learn; however, the trick is in being able to walk the fine line between a *too* soft question (which causes television viewers to shout at the screen, "Why don't you ask a *real* question?!") and a *sort of* soft question, such as, "Mr. Prime Minister, what is your favorite breakfast cereal?" (We told you it was a fine line.)

It is recommended that you practice as a family, yelling "Soft!" every time a question is asked that is too complex or requires too much thought.

There is, of course, a downside to your insisting that all the questions your teen ask be soft. Unfortunately, he will never be able to ask you about that dope, or whether it's safe to drink and drive or have unprotected sex. But this will work itself out.

Final Preparations

You're just about done! If you've followed our instructions to the letter, your little Anchor-to-Be should be about ready for his first job interview. Since the road to the top rarely runs through Fargo, you will be planning your move to a *major city*. It is important that you move along with your child since he will have to live at home during the first decade or so of abysmal entry-level TV journalism pay.

During this time, you will, of course, continue to offer your guidance and advice. Yes—even though you have accomplished the difficult parts of raising your Anchor-to-Be, there's still plenty of work ahead.

And don't lose hope if his first on-screen position is Weatherperson (or, God forbid, Sports Announcer!). Nobody starts at the top. Not even your child. But yours *will* get there faster than the rest.

Raising Your Child to Become a
Stewardess!

Degree of Difficulty
9.2

More difficult than raising a Pope, raising a Stewardess is not as easy as you think! It's a major challenge raising someone who can push all those carts around while dealing with morons who always decide to go to the bathroom right during cocktail service. Unless you're up for some difficult parenting, perhaps you should try raising a pilot. It's much easier.

But if you're up to the challenge, let's get started. And think of how good you'll feel, doing your bit to make the skies even friendlier!

Cost of Upbringing	Income Potential	Cost/Income Ratio
$	$$$$	**4.6** (1–10) Higher is better

The New, Hot Profession

Few people know (except for readers of this book) what a great professional choice this is. And the reason? There's little left to do in the way of actual work! In the '50s and '60s, stewardesses were trudging down the aisle serving free cocktails, being overly polite, and asking if you wanted steak au poirve, chicken cordon bleu, or pasta primavera for your main course (oops, "And what kind of salad dressing would you like?").

Now their job description is: throw passengers a bag of Fritos and head back to the crew rest seats for a long nap. Nice work, if you can get it. Let those factory workers put in the full eight hour days, performing the same mindless tasks over and over. Your child can cruise through life if you follow our instructions.

And your little one will thank you for providing her with a profession that allows her to work well into her eighties. No matter how many miles she has on her, she'll keep flying so her husband can use those free passes to go to Vegas with his golfing buddies every year (he retired years ago). If she wobbles a bit while traveling down the aisle, she's confident that her seniority will keep her in the air and keep the kind of cute young thing who used to serve us waiting tables at Hooters until there's finally a job opening.

105

When your little Stewardess-to-Be arrives home from the hospital, you will want to make sure you've done your preflight checkup so that her nursery is prepared in the proper manner. Make sure her boarding pass is in order, and prepare the room as shown below.

In the cradle
- Seat belts
- Oxygen mask
- Barf bags
- Baby bottle "miniatures"

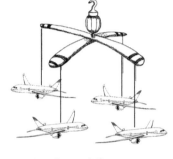

In the toy box
- Plastic wings from your last flight
- DVDs of *Airplane!* and *Airport*

On the mobile
- Planes, planes, planes

On the wall
- Framed autographed photo of Lloyd Bridges
- Last known photo of Howard Hughes

Home Tutoring

Although your local school may be excellent, it's up to you to concentrate your efforts in areas specifically relating to your daughter's career. In addition to specialized math training (see below) and vocabulary, you would be wise not to forget training her in *proper table service!*

Vocabulary
- Welcome aboard
- Pretzels or chips?
- Can't you see I'm *busy!*
- Bu-bye, bu-bye

Math Exercises
Important! She will need to understand numbers so that when her pension is yanked out from under her, she knows exactly how much she has lost.

Recommended Reading
- *Coffee, Tea, or Me?*
- *Turbulence: The Essential Guide to Becoming a Flight Attendant*
- *Stewardess: Come Fly with Me*

Stewardess or Flight Attendant?
P.C. in the Skies

For most of the '90s, the term Flight Attendant became the politically correct term and Stewardess fell out of favor and became politically incorrect.

Stewardesses (we mean Flight Attendants) bristled at the term. But suddenly, as their jobs grew more boring and their passengers more unruly, they started longing for the good old days of *Coffee, Tea, or Me?* They remembered when their friends said "Oh, you're a stewardess. Lucky you! It must be so exciting flying all over the world and meeting rich and sophisticated passengers." So they began using the term again in hopes of getting some of the magic back. One can always dream.

Rumor has it they would even consider going back to "Air Hostess" if necessary.

Parents who have not had the good sense to purchase this book will understandably think that a multitude of exciting travel posters is the proper decoration for a Stewardess-to-Be's room. However, this will simply build unrealizable expectations, since she won't have the time between landing and takeoff to see anything but the inside of a hotel room to take a quick nap. The wall decorations below will be far better at preparing her for flying countless hours in an aluminum tube with nothing to look at through those tiny windows but clouds.

Incorrect wall decor

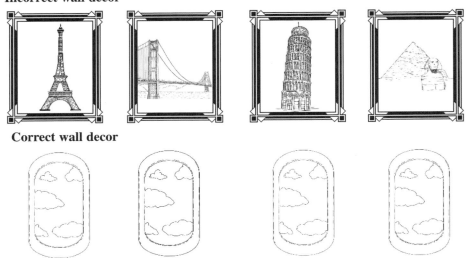

Correct wall decor

Early Attire
The Dork Factor

Fortunately, you will not have to spend a fortune on a wardrobe for your child. You'll save tons of money by shopping at resale shops, where the selection of out-of-style fashions is never ending. The key is to get her used to wearing out-of-date, dorky clothes, so that when she is presented with her first uniform, she does not recoil in horror (as her passengers certainly will). Before long, she'll be perfectly comfortable wearing her ten-year-older sister's cast offs.

And while her classmates are

ruining their feet (and clubbing it) with those sexy, strappy, spiked heels, your little darling will be perfectly happy in her "sensible" shoes. And best of all, she'll thank you for it when she's eighty.

Editor's Cautionary Note
Best New Name for a Plane

Boeing doesn't get it. Or maybe they don't want to admit they do. "767," "727," "Dreamliner"? These names might sound great from a marketing standpoint, but do they really describe what flying has become? No. We left it up to the French (who think marketing is what you do when you buy groceries) to come up with the perfect name for airliners of today: "Airbus."

Get in line, step lively, climb on board in your T-shirts and cargo pants. Caution your Stewardess-to-Be: it's not like the good old days!

Smart parents prepare their Stewardess-to-Be by adding an emergency slide to their house for important practice. And it's fun, too. All the neighborhood kids will want to give it a try!

The Formative Years

Possibly the most important training you can give your little Stewardess-to-Be is to teach her to ignore rude and obnoxious behavior. Luckily for you, this is best accomplished by being rude and obnoxious to her through her early years and beyond. She'll get used to it.

And, oh, will your friends be jealous! They have to be sweet to their little brats. They have to be nice and understanding, even through the terrible teen years, while you won't.

This is what we mean when we say raising a Stewardess is one of the more difficult parenting jobs. You will find there will actually be times (rarely) when you will want to be pleasant to your child. It is difficult, *but you must resist the urge!*

She will thank you for it later when a passenger tugs at her skirt and demands, "Where's my free drink?" and she confidently replies, "When you're done dining at a restaurant, you're still in the same place where you started. Now you're on a plane. You get food *and* a trip. They can't *both* be great. Get a life!"

Valuable Tip

If you are lucky enough to live near a sports stadium, your child may be able to land one of those coveted summer jobs that will go a long way in preparing her for that Stewardess career. A hot dog, soft drink, or beer vendor position will teach the invaluable skills necessary to excel in the air. (Airlines tend to frown at Stewardesses who throw food to their passengers, which is why Peanut Vendor is not a desirable position.)

Raising Your Child to Become a
King/Queen!*

* Includes Emperor
and Empress

**Degree of Difficulty
8.5**

King? Queen? Okay, this is a tough one, but certainly not impossible, as the following pages will show. The trick is to get your child to Prince or Princess level—then she's on her own—hoping she's next in line and the right people kick the bucket.

And getting to Prince or Princess isn't all that difficult, since it generally requires simply marrying well.

Not that many royals out there, you say? Think again. Just because a country doesn't have sitting royalty doesn't mean it doesn't have a pretender somewhere just waiting for his subjects to call him back. Even Albania has a king. And Italy! (Somewhere)

With that many Kings and Queens floating around, you just know there are lots of Princes and Princesses, as well. Just follow our advice and we guarantee that your Superchild will land one of his or her very own.

Cost of Upbringing	Income Potential	Cost/Income Ratio
$$$	$$$$$$$$$	**9.3** (1–10) Higher is better

Is It Really Possible?

Rest assured that your little Prince- or Princess-to-Be really *does* have a shot at the big time. The barriers are coming down in even the stodgiest of monarchies. The Japanese royal family, for example—the oldest in the world—recently let a commoner into the fold when the current empress, Michiko Shoda, married Crown Prince Akihito in 1959. She was the first commoner ever to enter the family.

The Crown Prince became emperor in 1989 and presto, our little commoner became empress!

And let's not forget that scrub woman, Cinderella, who stole the heart of the handsome Prince and made it to the top.

Proper Attire

Although the public doesn't get to vote on a bride- or groom-to-be when he or she is marrying into a royal family, most royals take public opinion into consideration. And the Swedish Act of Succession states that a prince or princess of the Royal House may not marry unless the government has given its consent. So here are some tips.

Girls: Be hot enough to attract the Prince's attention when he's out clubbin', but not so hot that you will fail to pass muster with the Mr. & Mrs. King and Queen. Hooter's attire is out. Dressing like a kindergarten teacher is okay.

Guys: Attire is not as important as a good job (or the appearance of one). Banking will do nicely. Pool boy will not.

113

The Early Years—Preparing Your Royal-to-Be's Room

If she's going to "bust into" royalty, you need to get her off to the right start. Paint the room in shades of royal blue and play "Don't Cry for Me Argentina" to lull her to sleep.

In the crib
- Stuffed Snow White doll
- *The Princess and the Pea* (for bedtime reading)
- Pea

Grace Kelly

Eva Perón

Princess Diana

Royalty Busters Trading Cards
Collect 'em, trade 'em. They'll keep your little one motivated

Pass
Lifetime free pass to Disneyland

FREE!
Good Forever

Playhouse
Miniature castle (moat optional)

For the DVD player
- *Snow White*
- *The King and I*
- *Evita!*
- *The Grace Kelly Story*
- Nothing with Queen Latifah

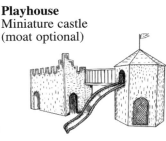

Increasing Your Child's Chances

If your child is to succeed in her quest, it is your job to understand how marriage patterns in various countries with monarchies can have a big impact on her chances of landing the "big one."

If you remain a resident of the United States, your chances of landing a Royal will be slim. It's just that we don't have a lot of real Royals running around. We have a few "pretenders," although they generally prefer Monaco for the tax advantages. So you may have to move to a strange country, but, hey, what's having to change your religion or learn Farsi or Urdu when it comes to your child's future well-being?

Note: What is a pretender? A good example is Luis Alfonso de Borbon, who lives in Venezuela. He claims he is the rightful King of France, since his family's bloodlines lead back to Luis XX. If your daughter married him, her chances of wearing the crown are slim, but at least she'd be rich. In the meantime, she can pretend.

It's a numbers game, actually. Countries with polygamous monarchies are the most fertile hunting grounds. After all, just one King with four wives could get you maybe sixteen to twenty potential Princes/Princesses in just the first generation. After a few generations, you've got a couple hundred floating around, *all in need of spouses!* Monogamous monarchies, like those in Sweden and England, pump their Royals out one or two at a time, greatly decreasing your child's chances.

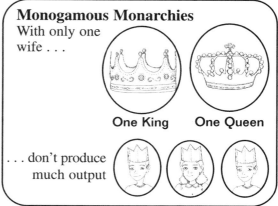

Monogamous Monarchies
With only one wife . . .

One King   One Queen

. . . don't produce much output

Polygamous Monarchies

Lots of wives means lots of available Princes and Princesses.

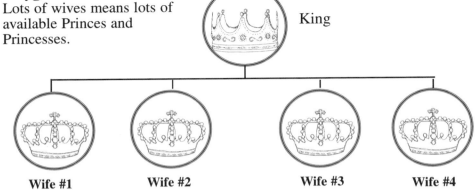

King

Wife #1   Wife #2   Wife #3   Wife #4

First batch of Princes/Princesses

Within a few years, wow! Hundreds to choose from!

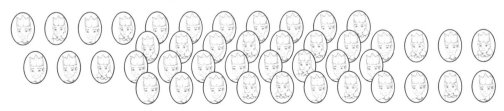

Should you settle for a pretender to a title or go for the gold and try to join the family of a real sitting monarch? There are advantages and disadvantages to both. To become "Royal" by marrying into a pretender's family basically all you get is a title (which isn't too bad), but latch on to a real sitting monarch's offspring and you get all the good stuff, like castles and footmen. Which is best for your child? See our handy chart below.

Benefit	Sitting Monarchy	Pretender to the Throne
Title?	Yes	Yes, but it's a pretend one
Throne?	Yes	Only in your bathroom
Boring royal duties?	Way too many	Thankfully, no
Salary?	Yes, but not like it used to be	Better get a job
Servants?	Depending on country. Denmark, no; Togo, yes	Only hangers-on
Jewels?	Tiaras for the ladies. Guys get crowns and nifty cufflinks (and, oh, those cool sashes!)	Only what's left after selling off most of the grandma's stuff to meet living expenses; guys still get cool sashes.
Tabloid coverage?	Too much	Just enough so you feel famous
Paparazzi?	Get ready!	Thankfully, none
Bragging rights?	Plenty!	???????

117

"Hey look, they're 'one of us'!"

Nose Training: The Appropriate Angle

Most Americans, upon meeting someone for the first time, do not pay attention to her nose angle. However, as a parent of a Royal-to-Be, you had better get used to it. If your child is going to "bump into" royalty at that charity auction or ribbon-cutting ceremony for that new sewage plant, she will need to look like "one of our kind." Your kid is going to have to get the nose angle thing down pat if she is to have a chance of hooking a Royal.

Most parents are a bit naive and think a simple nose job will do the trick. But let us set you straight. It won't.

On the other hand, this is not brain surgery. If Charles can do it, so can your kid. Get a plumb bob from your local hardware store and hang it from her nose until that 12 degrees feels natural. And that "drowning in a rainstorm" thing is just an urban legend.

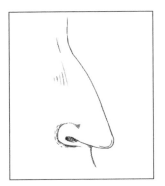

0°—Looking straight
Unacceptable

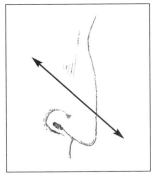

12°—Looking down
Unacceptable

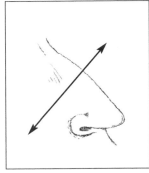

-12°—Looking up (Royal)
Acceptable

118

How to Make an Aluminum Foil Crown

Getting your little loved one to become accustomed to wearing the Royal Crown is critical. The proper balance and poise are to be learned early in life. This is the sort of subliminal child-rearing technique that can make the difference between "possible" Queen and "always a commoner." *For a complete how-to video demonstration, click on YouTube.com/niftytiara.* Note: For best results, this activity should be combined with Nose Training (see previous page).

Step 1. Take a 1 foot square sheet of aluminum foil.

Step 2. Fold flap B over flap C and flap G.

Step 3. Unfold quickly and, it's a miracle, the perfect proper Royal Tiara!

Shown: Incorrect folds can result in an inaccurate representation of hat. Try again.

One Last Thought
The Homeliness Factor
People think everyone wants to marry into royalty, but the truth is, once they get a good look at some of them, they change their minds. So your child's competition isn't quite as stiff as you might think. It's a sad fact of royal life, but all that inbreeding produces some pretty homely (and pretty boring) offspring. This is to your child's advantage because, based on our advice, you will raise her to have looks and personality fairly far down on her list of priorities in a mate.

Raising Your Child to Become an
International Wine Connoisseur!

Degree of Difficulty
4.4

Wow! Getting paid to drink! And not just any old swill, but the really good stuff, too—thousand-dollar bottles of wine!

You're probably wishing you'd have known about this "profession" when you were younger; it could have altered your own career path. Well, you may have missed the boat, but your child doesn't have to. If you raise him right, instead of punching a clock, he'll be poppin' corks and bringing in big bucks just for saying, "Hey, that's not bad. I'll give it a nine point five."

So grab your corkscrew and let's get started. We guarantee that your child will thank you for it. And what does he have to lose (except his liver)?

Cost of Upbringing	Income Potential	Cost/Income Ratio
$$	$$$$$	**5.8** (1–10) Higher is better

Have you thought this through? *Points to consider:*	
<u>Pros</u>	<u>Cons</u>
Paid for drinking ⟶	None
Have to drink every day ⟶	See below*
Don't pay for the good stuff ⟶	Have to taste the rotgut, too
No heavy lifting ⟶	* No liver

If your child shows no aptitude for study or hard work, becoming an International Wine Connoisseur may be his ticket.

And here's the good news: *nobody* can actually tell the difference between a $10 bottle of wine and a $1,000 bottle. So your child won't have to learn a lot. He will, however, have to learn to *pretend*.

Most people think the requirements for such a lofty profession are well-trained taste buds, a sophisticated palate, and an excellent sense of smell. Wrong! More important than the *taste* of wine on his tongue will be his ability to make *flowery phrases* roll off it. Before you're done with his upbringing he'll be spouting ". . . aromas of smoke, sausage, bacon, blue-berry, and tar rise from the glass... supple and ripe on the palate . . . full-bodied and well-structured . . ." Wow!

The Early Years
Your budding oenophile won't have to wait until he is twenty-one before he begins serious training in wine tasting. Instead of buying expensive wine for him to taste in his preteen years, you'll be providing him with the crucial plastic, bacon, tar, oak, vanilla, charcoal, berries, and minerals they will need to taste to succeed.

Author's Note: It is not considered wise to allow your in-laws to see you feeding plastic or tar to your child.

When your little one grows up, he will be spending a lot of time in dark, dank wine cellars, so it helps to get him acclimated early. Prepare his room by getting rid of any excess lighting, keeping necessary lighting to a minimum and setting the thermostat to a red-wine-friendly 55°F, and whatever you do, don't remove those cobwebs!

Cradle
• Made from Limousin oak wine cask

In the toy box
• Crayons (Limited to 3 colors: Red, White, and Rose´)
• DVD of *Sideways*

Baby bottles
• Stored in temperature-controlled wine rack

Bordeaux			
1960 ***	1976 ***	1992 ***	***
1961 **	1977 ***	1993 **	***
1962 ***	1978 ***	1994 **	***
1963 ***	1979 ***	1995 **	***
1964 ***	1980 ***	1996 ***	**
1965 ***	1981 **	1997 ***	***
1966 ***	1982 ***	1998 **	
1967 **	1983 ***	1999 **	***
1968 ***	1984 **	2000 ***	***
1969 ***	1985 ***	2001 **	***
1970 **	1986 ***	2002 ***	***
1971 **	1987 **	2003 ***	**
1972 **	1988 ***	2004 **	**
1973 ***	1989 ***	2005 ***	***
1974 **	1990 **	2006 **	
1975 **	1991 ***	2007 **	

On the wall
• Framed autographed photo of Robert Parker
• Bordeaux vintage charts covering the last 150 years

What the heck is a palate?

Actually, there is no such thing as a palate. A history lesson is in order here. Back in the early 1800s, a famous wine taster was writing in his blog about how he spilled some very expensive wine onto his plate, and he drank it anyway, and it tasted great. Unfortunately, he misspelled "plate," and the comment read: ". . . it tasted great on my *palate*."

Wine tasters everywhere, eager as always to follow a new trend, assumed he had discovered the key to being a well-respected connoisseur and posted stories of how their palates, too, were producing exceptional tastes. Soon the average peasant, not wishing to appear the fool for not having a good palate, helped spread the word far and wide. The term remains with us today; however, the true International Wine Connoisseur knows he is just perpetuating an urban legend when he brags about how sensitive his palate is.

This is a true story.

Only the Nose Knows

Early Training

Since we now know that the palate does not exist, what, you might ask, is the part of the body that allows us to experience the true joys of wine? It is, dear parent, the nose! And we have learned this from the French, along with numerous other important things, such as how to enjoy stinky cheese.

The French have paid the price for being the preeminent wine-producing country in the world: it is their rather "robust" probosci that got them there. This appendage has evolved into the perfect wine-sniffing machine, which is the reason why all International Wine Connoisseurs share this ungainly shape. What to do if your IWC-to-Be does not possess such a snout? The

Typical French
Nose

Typical Wine
Connoisseur's Nose

125

recommended procedure is to enlarge it, commonly known as proboscis augmentation.

Some parents are repelled by this procedure; however, it is rather simple, less expensive than a nose job, and perfectly safe, if the proper tool is used.

Often mistaken for a wine opener or corkscrew, the device shown below

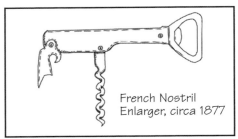

French Nostril Enlarger, circa 1877

is actually a nostril enlarger. Invented by the French right after they blessed the world with the guillotine, this handy tool has been used by amateur and professional wine tasters alike for decades. Your child should sleep with it inserted (Caution: two turns only!) in his nose for the first three years of his life.

Home Tutoring

Get out your dictionary! Although your little Wine Connoisseur will be taking theater and acting classes in school, it's up to you to make sure he learns the necessary polysyllabic words that will make him a star.

It's your job to select and circle these impressive words in the dictionary. Your child must learn that saying "good" or "great" is not enough to move up in the international big-time wine circles. He will need mighty impressive words and phrases to throw around.

Vocabulary
Jammy, citrusy, austere, heady, structured, voluptuous, syrupy, lusty, silly, fanciful, red, white, sort of pink, sparkling, tickles my nose

Playtime!

Playing "Pretend"

All kids love to play "Pretend," so your job is easy. Encourage your child to play as frequently as possible while teaching him various pretentious phrases (see next page).

Even when he reaches adulthood and becomes a true Connoisseur, he won't be able to tell the difference between a Two-Buck Chuck and Petrus '47, so pretending will become invaluable.

Swallowing is acceptable.
Chugging is not.

Nice Children Don't Spit (or Do They?)

While parents everywhere are faced with the seemingly impossible task of teaching their children *not* to spit ("Stop that! Polite people don't spit!"), the fortunate parents of International Wine Connoisseurs-to-Be are faced with a much more difficult task: teaching their children to spit *properly*.

But it's not that easy. There's the fairly easy *common* spit and the much more difficult *fake* spit.

To Common Spit or to Fake Spit?

If you want your child to advance beyond the mere everyday wine expert to the realm of the true International Wine Connoisseur, you must teach him the little-known art of the *Sip/Swirl/Fake Spit*.

The reason most wine experts can't tell the difference between Château Rothschild and Château Rotgut is that they have been taught to spit out the wine after flamboyantly swirling it around in their mouths. This is supposedly to prevent them from getting drunk during a typical day of tasting hundreds of wines.

A true *International* Wine Connoisseur, however, knows that this is hogwash for two reasons: first, the true taste buds are way, way, way down in the throat and, second, getting tipsy, or even downright drunk, is half the fun.

Therefore, it is important to *appear* to spit so observers don't realize that the taster is actually swallowing and fast becoming wiped out. Since the fake spit (devised by

Monsieur André Duval in the early 1800s) is even more difficult to perform correctly than is opening a wine bottle, we have prepared a twenty-minute demonstration video which can be seen at Youtube.com/dothefakespit.

The 3Ps
<u>P</u>ompous and <u>P</u>retentious <u>P</u>hrases

Most children learn the 3Rs. Your child will learn the 3Ps to prop up his fragile ego with wine pretensions, look down on people who drink wine that he considers "not up to snuff," and talk in a manner that demeans everyone not "in the know."

Get out the thesaurus. Teach him the value of the Pompous, and Pretentious Phrase. He must always ask himself . . .

Why say? . . .	**. . . when they can say:**
Not bad . . .	Plenty of berry fruit interwoven with notions of charcoal . . .
Smooth . . .	Possesses an overriding elegance . . .
Smells good . . .	Impeccably balanced, combined with a nose that is a floral infused effort . . .
They want *how much* for this stuff?!	It takes a true connoisseur to appreciate the nuances in this subtle example.

In conclusion—*A Fine Finish*
Even though you will be turning your child into a pompous ass, don't despair. The IRS lets you write off all that expensive wine you supposedly were buying for his education but were drinking yourself (while he munched on that plastic and tar).

Raising Your Child to Become a
Rock Star!

Degree of Difficulty
5.0

So you *want to be a Rock Star?* Well sex, drugs, and rock & roll can all be yours (vicariously, of course) if you prepare your child for one of the most popular of all super professions: Rock Star!

And we don't mean some run-of-the mill, "Idol" type star. We're talkin' the serious, single-name variety. Think Elvis, Madonna, Elton, Sting, or even, yes, Bono or Pink. So hire an architect for that home addition. You're going to need more wall space to display all those platinum albums and more bedrooms to house the hoards of groupies. Fame for your little one, fame for *you*. Get ready to see his picture on the cover of *Rolling Stone*!

Cost of Upbringing	Income Potential	Cost/Income Ratio
$$$	$$$$$$$$$$	**9.2** (1–10) Higher is better

The Early Years

A quick look (or should we say listen) around at what's out there in the rock world should tell you that your little one's not going to need a lot of real talent to climb to the top. Plenty of Holiday Inn lounge singers can sing better than Madonna. And if he can't sing at all? No problem. Lip synchers have been known to win a Grammy.

So what *is* the key to the Rock Star's success? *Attitude!* And it's your job, dear parent, to instill a proper one early in life (unless, of course, you want him to sell out, go corporate, and strive to have his biggest hit turned into the theme for a Ford commercial. But that's a different story).

Where to start? Well, a good place would be the Seven Deadly Sins, all of which are necessary to create the perfect attitude. Of course, in addition to the basics of lust, greed, sloth, etc., we would add arrogance and "strutability." No humility here! And best of all, you'll discover that these traits are not difficult to develop in your child.

As a parent, you should feel a sense of relief. Whew—this won't be as hard as you thought. While all your friends and neighbors are desperately trying to raise nice, sweet, responsible kids (what a chore that must be!), you'll have it easy.

So download Nickelback's *I Want to Be a Rockstar* (the unedited version, of course) to your little one's iPod, crank up the volume, and let's get the show on the road!

The Early Years—Preparing Your Rock Star-to-Be's Room

The most important furnishing in your little one's room will be the cot you place there for you to sleep on. You'll want to be close by all through the night so you can comfort him at the first sign of distress. He should learn early in life there will always be someone nearby to cater to his every whim. God forbid he should suffer!

In the cradle
- *Book of 1,001 Best Tattoos*
- *I'm with the Band: Confessions of a Groupie*, by Pamela Des Barres
- *AC/DC: Maximum Rock & Roll: The Ultimate Story of the World's Greatest Rock-and-Roll Band*, by Murray Engleheart

In the DVD player
- *School of Rock*
- Stones' Altamont concert documentary
- *The Wall*
- *Tommy*

In the medicine cabinet
- For her: hair dye, heavy eye liner, black nail polish
- For him: hair dye, heavy eye liner, black nail polish

On the wall
- For her: Autographed poster of Beatles or Lazy Angels
- For him: Autographed photo of Pamela Anderson

Choosing the Right Instrument

We do not recommend you waste your money on voice lessons. If your little one learns to play an instrument, he won't really have to be much of a singer. (Or he could skip the instrument, too, and just become a rapper, in which case he wouldn't have to be much of a singer either.)

Your child's choice of instrument can be important. It can determine the degree of stardom he will achieve. Be fore-warned! The road to fame and fortune is strewn with parents insisting the kazoo was rock & roll's instrument of the future. Don't make this mistake.

As the chart below shows, there are only three instruments that lead directly to rock stardom: the guitar (air included), piano, and drums. Each has it's advantages and proponents.

There are, of course, instances where other, more obscure instruments have lead to stardom: the saxophone (think

Instrument	Degree of Difficulty	Comment
* Guitar	7	The King!
* Piano	9	Hard to jump around
Accordion	4	For Milwaukee Rock Stars
Harp	12	Heaven can wait. Only good for soft rock
* Drums	3	If Ringo can learn to play them, so can your kid
Kazoo	1	Yeah, sure
Triangle	0	Only if you name your kid Isosceles

* Recommended

Bill Clinton), the banjo (think Steve Martin), and the ukulele (think Pee Wee Herman) come to mind. But these cases are relatively rare, which is why we recommend sticking with the big three. And they're easy to learn, too!

If your little Rock Star-to-Be lacks finger-to-keyboard or finger-to-guitar string coordination, they can always learn to play the drums. It's been said that if 10,000 monkeys (not the band) banged on drums for a thousand years, they would end up composing a Ringo Starr solo.

Lyrics

Children's books with simplistic plot lines and basic rhymes will be sufficient to help you train your little Rock Star-to-Be for the difficult task of writing profound lyrics. No matter how inane the words he writes, his rock critics will always assign some deep, hidden meaning. And most fans won't be able to understand the lyrics, anyway.

Home Tutoring

A formal education isn't going to help much, so it's up to you to provide proper guidance. Since your little one will be learning an instrument instead of how to read, you'll have to do the studying. The following recommended books are for *you* (your little one can tackle them when he reaches twenty-one and have finally learned to read the "big words").

Recommended Reading for You:
The Dirt: Confessions of the World's Most Notorious Rock Band by Tommy Lee, Vince Neil, Mick Mars, and Nikki Sixx; *Hooks That Kill - The Best of Mick Mars and Motley Crue* by Motley Crue and Mick Mars; and *Motley Crue: Lewd, Crude & Rude* by Sylvie Simmons, *Kiss Kiss Bang Bang*, by Gene Simmons

Recommended Reading for Him:
The Rhyming Dictionary

Stimulating Childhood Activities
The Field Trip

Here's a fun activity for all concerned and one that's educational as well. While other parents are taking their little ones camping in the wild, you will be enjoying luxurious surroundings complete with spa, room service, and a concierge, because you're heading for the poshest hotel in town for a weekend stay. Don't worry about the expense because you're going to skip out on the bill (to set the right example).

Your only out-of-pocket costs for these fun trips will be for a few guitars. Buy them at the Salvation Army store or local garage sales because your little Rock Star-to-Be will be throwing them through the windows and off the balcony. Invite your kid's underage friends to join you for a night of revelry. It's important for him to get used to groupies. And don't forget to trash the room. We told you it would be fun!

These educational field trips should start around the age of seven or eight years old and continue through his teenage years. By that time everyone in his band should have fake IDs and they can go unsupervised.

We are frequently asked if it is really necessary to conduct so many of these field trips when most kids seem to learn quickly what is expected of them. Actually, it's not really necessary to plan more than two or three of these excursions, but they allow you to spend quality time with your tyke, and they're a chance to get out of the house and have someone else clean and cook for you. We're sure, from a parenting standpoint at least, this is why more is better.

The Downside
Only the "Good" Die Young

There is a minor problem when raising a Rock (or Movie) Star: as a result of long-term drug and/or alcohol use, they tend to kick the bucket a bit earlier than the average citizen.

A recent scientific study showed that Elvis Presley, Jim Morrison, Kurt Cobain, Janis Joplin, and Jimi Hendrix are no longer with us. Not only that; they left us way before they probably wanted to.

Of course if your kid is not very "good," he might live longer but then, he wouldn't be a Rock Star, just a rocker. Anyway, as we said, it's a minor problem.

RIP

- **Janis Joplin, 27** • **Jim Morrison, 27**
- **Jimi Hendrix, 27** • **Marilyn Monroe, 36**
- **Tupac Shakur, 25** • **James Dean, 24**
- **Kurt Cobain, 27**

The Mick Effect

Since you will be paying your child's bills until he hits it big, you'll be happy to know there will be no need for cosmetic surgery. This will save you tons of money. At fifteen the "Mick Effect" will take over and he will remain ageless. Trust us. If he leads a typical rock star's lifestyle he won't age between fifteen and eighty-five.

Mick at thirteen

Mick at fifteen

Mick at eighty-five?

Conclusion
The American Idol Myth

Our recommendation is: skip it. Why take the difficult road to success, slogging through weeks of competition trying to impress what's-his-name? Why suffer through the humiliation? (Unless your kid's after that Ford commercial). After all, how many albums or CDs did Simon Cowell buy last year?

Raising Your Child to Become an
International
Art Forger!

**Degree of Difficulty
3.2**

Admit it, you say it every time you look at a Picasso: "Even *I* could do that!" And the sad part is, yes, you could! Face it, *anybody could*! But you didn't, and you missed your chance. But it's not too late for Junior. With our expert advice and the cost of a few crayons and some finger paints, your child could end up filthy rich just for cranking out one or two measly works of "art" a year. Counterfeiting, you say. Isn't that wrong? It's not counterfeiting when it's art. And if nobody can tell the difference, what's the harm?!

Cost of Upbringing	Income Potential	Cost/Income Ratio
$$	$$$$$$$$$$	**9.6** (1–10) Higher is better

Pros	Cons
Paint masterpieces ⟶	Don't get credit
Messy work ⟶	Acrylics clean up easily
Get to wear a beret ⟶	Get to wear a beret
Big bucks ⟶	Won't get NEA grant

Copying the Masters

If your little one is going to make a living by forging works of art, we recommend he forge artists who people have actually heard of. Trust us, it will be much more lucrative. Following are some examples of famous original artworks and both successful and unsuccessful fakes. You will note it is important to teach your little International Art Forger-to-Be to carefully study the style and ideocyncracies of each artist he is attempting to copy. Little things, like the use of color, size of brushstroke, and correct signature will make the difference between a forgery that will only pass scrutiny on eBay and one that will fool Scotland Yard or a competent international art dealer (if you can find one). We've also scattered technical tips throughout this chapter. Please make sure your little Forger-to-Be understands them completely.

Fooling the Experts

As you will soon discover, art dealers really know their stuff (they just don't know a lot about art) and so do billionaire art collectors who only three years ago were still collecting baseball cards.

But it's not impossible to fool either group. So all in all, this is a pretty good gig if you just follow our advice and teach your little tyke some basic tricks of the trade.

The way in which you decorate and furnish your little one's room will help determine which artist he will emulate (copy) later in life. So the good news is, it's entirely up to you.

Messy and you're raising a Pollack; lots of fun-house mirrors, a Warhol; bold colors, a Calder; and pastels, you've got a little Monet on your hands.

In the toy box
• Crayons, crayons, crayons!

Scattered about
• Nothing but counterfeits. Louis Vuittons and Oakleys, etc. He has to learn early that the only difference is the price.

On the wall
• No master artworks here, just framed auto-graphed photo of TV's fastest painter, Jerry Yarnell!
• Washable wallpaper for doodling

In the cradle
• Canvas sheets and blankets. He'll get used to it.

Copying a Mondrian

An authentic Mondrian (Fig. 1) is not difficult to copy if you follow our instructions. Don't be discouraged by your little Forger-to-Be's first attempt (Fig. 2) when he is only three months old. By the time he is six or seven

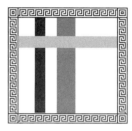

Fig. 1
Original
Value $6,000,000

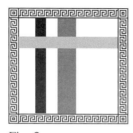

Fig. 2
Fake
Value $0

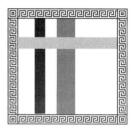

Fig. 3
Fake
Value $6,000,000

years old, he should have mastered the balance and structure that are the mark of a true genius, or a true forger (Fig. 3).

Good art dealers or filthy rich international collectors will be able to spot the amateur attempt shown in Fig. 2—or is it Fig. 3? Well, trust us, *they* can tell.

Copying a Picasso

Note the precise brushstrokes (Fig. 4, following page), which is obviously an original. The forger (who shall remain unnamed) followed Picasso's style exactly and produced this fake (Fig. 5), which fooled art dealers worldwide as well as both Scotland Yard and the FBI. When it was unveiled as a fake, all concerned said: "Gee, you coulda fooled us. It sure looks like a Picasso!"

Tip No. 2
Do Not Paint Objects
Upside Down.
Unless you're copying a Picasso

Fig. 4 Original
Value $32,000,000

Fig. 5 Superb copy
Value $32,000,000

Choosing the Easiest

Inept forgers often make the mistake of attempting to copy art from the Realism School (so named because the paintings look real), as opposed to the silly (so named for the Sillyism School). It is far more difficult to copy a painting that actually resembles something. So stick to abstract works.

However, such a scam *can* be accomplished if the forger has a great degree of skill, as is shown in the example here. When copying the painting of this exceptional landscape (Fig. 6), the forger was able to fool the experts by matching the original artist's style perfectly (Fig. 7). To the untrained (non-art dealer) eye, they look identical. As you might understand, not only amateurs, like you and me, were fooled.

Fig. 6
Real
Value $14,000,000

Fig. 7
Fake
Value $14,000,000

Tip No. 3
Stick with Copying Abstract Art;
Avoid the More Difficult Realism.

Tools of the Trade

The good news is this profession does not require a large expenditure on the part of the parents for specialized tools or equipment.

Readers have reported they used leftover rollers, brushes, and even paint from their last kitchen remodeling with great success.

Our studies here at the Institute have shown that Benjamin Moore works best for pre-nineteenth-century forgeries, Behr for later works.

Your Friends the Art Dealers

It's not fair that art dealers are accused of fraud when they sell all those fakes. This assumes they actually *knew* the art were fakes when most can't tell the difference between a Kinkade and a Kandinsky.

Most art dealers will (unwittingly) be your child's friends; however, it will be important for your kid to be selective. Teach your child to listen, not look, when interviewing a dealer he plans to scam. He will be able to tell whether dealers are competent simply by their vocabulary. When describing one of their paintings on display, if they say, "I think it's pretty," your child should know to move on; they know their stuff! What your child should be looking for is someone who might say, ". . . therefore, we rediscover that Pre-Raphaelitism claimed to strip away 'sentimentality' and 'mannerism' from this work." Go for the jugular!

And keep in mind that art dealers know signatures. Many a forger (whose parents did not have the foresight to purchase this book) has been tripped up by the smallest of details, like the signature. Sure, it's tough to fool these guys, but careful attention to detail will save the day.

Tip No. 4
When Signing the Painting, Always Spell the Artist's Name Correctly.

Your Friends the Nouveau Rich

As Fitzgerald said, "The rich are different from you and me; they're not as smart." Well, that's what he *meant* to say, at least about the new ones, or as they like to refer to themselves, the "nouveau" ones. We refer to them as "easy marks." And not only are they easier to scam, but also they have the big bucks that make it all worthwhile.

Teach your child that "the newer the money, the easier they fall" and to stay away from old money.

The best way to practice when your kid is young is to sell their works on eBay. Not only will their works be subject to the scrutiny of millions of art "experts," but also once they earn that coveted four-star rating, you'll know they're ready for the big time.

Tip No. 5
When Forging Seventeenth-Century Masters, Do Not Use Markers.

The Importance of Provenance

If you're really hooked on the notion that your kid should get rich in the fake art field, yet he can't paint worth a hoot, there's still hope. You could train him to concentrate his efforts on creating phony provenances (or, as a last resort, he could just specialize in fake Jasper Johns works, although most successful art forgers consider that to be taking the easy way out).

Just because your little tyke was cooing Da-Da at birth doesn't mean he will learn how to paint it convincingly. But professionally done phony provenances can help sell that Man Ray even though it may look a bit suspect.

Phony provenances are simply one more tool your child can use to help everyone believe. And that's what it's all about, isn't it? While it may be hard to believe that $10,000,000.00 Miro you're getting for $5,000.00 is authentic, a neatly done provenance proving it came from

144

the Bill Gates collection will be all it takes to wrap up the sale.

A computer with a good word processing program and some clever typefaces are all that are needed to create some wonderfully authentic-looking provenances.

Of course, care should be taken, just as with fake paintings, to spell all names correctly.

> **Very Official Provenance**
>
> *My name is Bill Gates and I approve this painting.*

is that most of the work is already done for you! A closet full of hangers or a few light bulbs found around the house are all your little one will need. Spray them, mount them, sign them, sell them. Presto! There's a couple of mil.

Perfecting the Johns Joke

Contrary to popular belief, Jasper Johns is just one person (although parents lacking the sense to purchase this book will continue to believe he is a plural). And in addition to being just one person, he is widely believed in art forgery circles to be the easiest artist to forge this side of that guy who splatters paint all over.

If your little Forger-to-Be can't hack it in the Impressionist or even Post-Impressionist world, can't handle works from the Surrealists or Dadaists, Johns is the way to go.

The beauty of "creating" a Johns

Of course, as with any artist, there are pitfalls to avoid to ensure the most accurate reproduction. Please pay attention to Tip No. 6 below.

Tip No. 6
For Best Results When Creating a Jasper Johns, Do Not Use Compact Fluorescent Bulbs or Pant Hangers.

145

Conclusion

To avoid having your child grow up with a guilty conscience, it will be your job to place his or her new career in the proper prospective. As we mentioned earlier, people just want to believe, and your little one should develop a strong sense of satisfaction in helping them do so.

But above all, remind your child early and often that it's all about making art more affordable.

We also recommend you warn him to avoid the temptation to use his newfound talents to forge money, also known as "real" counterfeiting. This could get him into "real" trouble.

Tip No. 7
For Best Results, Do Not
Use a Copying Machine.

A Final Note from the Institute

Sometimes parents find it difficult to steer their child to a particular Super Profession. The kid will want to be a busboy, for example, and he'll complain, "It's too much work to make a lot of money. I'm just not that smart."

You won't have that problem steering your child to practice "Creative Reproduction" (as art forgery is known in polite circles). Simply open any art book and show him a Picassso. Point to it and say, "Twelve million bucks."

That should do it.

Raising Your Child to Become a
Bartender!

Degree of Difficulty
1.9

If it's been years since your favorite bartender bought you a drink "on the house," perhaps you should consider raising your own.

From a parenting standpoint, the amount of actual child-rearing work involved is miniscule (except for one problem area, but we'll get into that). And raising a bartender is cost-effective, too. No need to spend your hard-earned cash on special educational toys, or sock money away for a college education. The time frame is right, too. In as little as eighteen years (in some states), your kid can be earning six figures and pushing those freebies across the bar to good old mom and dad (don't forget to tip!).

Cost of Upbringing	Income Potential	Cost/Income Ratio
$	$$$$$	8.0 (1–10) Higher is better

147

148

Before You Start

Okay, let's get serious. This is a brief chapter, because, well, there's not a lot of parenting involved in creating this Super Profession.

Sure, there are other careers in which your child can make (lots) more money and that come with (a lot) more prestige, but if you're looking for the most bang for your buck, you can't go wrong in the world of the mixologist.

There's no large cash outlay needed for educational childhood toys or college tuition. And in some states, your kid can go right from high school to a six-figure income!

The job stability is fantastic, too. If your child gets fired for stealing from the till, there's always another bar down the block.

Home Tutoring

Not much to do here . . . Pop a *Cocktail* DVD in the player and read recipes from *Mr. Boston's Bartender's Guide* to him at bedtime. Some things, such as ducking behind the bar when the fights start, will be learned on the job.

Key phrases he will need to know:
"What can I getcha?"
"The usual?"
"This one's on me."
"You're cut off!"

The Early Years

We wouldn't want to suggest you start your little one on the "sauce" before he's of legal age, but he should be *exposed* to the stuff. And even though he can't legally serve before he's of

age, it's perfectly okay for him to act as your personal bartender as long as he stays on your premises.

So here it comes, the difficult part of raising your little tavern keeper, as we mentioned earlier. You're going to have to drink. A lot.

Your neighbors may recoil at seeing you stagger around in the middle of the day, but you should take comfort in the fact that you're preparing your little one for an exciting, lucrative career.

However, as difficult as this parenting might be, there are some benefits. Being served Bloody Marys every day for breakfast will not only give your little one good training, but it's also a great way to start the day! And there's more good news: here's your chance to be an obnoxious drunk for a good reason for a change.

And make sure cocktail hour is instructive, too, not only by drinking long and hard, but also by switching beverages frequently to test his recipe skills.

Finally, don't forget to stiff your little mixologist once in a while. It's good training for what he can expect in later years.

Coming of Age

Teach him early to live off his tips rather than an allowance. By the time he gets his first job it will be even harder to filch from the till; almost everything will be paid by credit card. Good for owners; bad for bartenders. Of course, there will always be scams to help your little one pad his paycheck. Even we can't keep up with the new ones, but not to worry—like ducking behind the bar, it's something else he'll learn quickly on the job.

And, once he gets his first job, your liquor bill will go down, since he'll be passing those freebies across the bar to you with reckless abandon.

Selecting His Venue

There are basically two types of bars/restaurants that your little Bartender-to-Be will work in: the Dive (or Shot and a Beer Joint) and the Classy (or Sophisticated Joint). Each has its advantages and disadvantages, as shown below.

Additionally, the Sophisticated Joint requires knowlege of vastly more complicated drinks, and therefore, more work. Prepare your little one for the joint of his choice by giving him proper in-home training so he has a head start over more disadvantaged youths with less concerned parents.

Shot and a Beer Joint	Sophisticated Joint
• Low-key clientele	• High-maintainence clientele
• Ordinary fights	• Catfights
• Five hundred $1 tips	• Fifty $10 tips
• No dress code	• Designer duds
• Football pools	• World Cup pools

Shot and a Beer Joint

It is critical that your child learn to instantly spot the difference between the glassware of choice in these establishments. This can be rather difficult, so we advise delaying your in-home training until he is at least in his teens. Note the subtle differences between the beer stein (Fig. 1) and the shot glass (Fig. 2).

Fig. 1

Fig. 2

Sophisticated Joint

The life of a bartender in a sophisticated joint is not all tap beers and gin and tonics. He will need to be prepared to mix more complicated drinks—such as a martini—and will need to demonstrate his ability to memorize detailed recipes and exhibit expert hand-to-glass coordination. If you think it's easy, consider these eye-opening points: 1. There are *two* ingredients to remember in a martini. 2. If you forget one, it's okay. 3. You have to pour *both* ingredients into a glass, while remembering to ask, "Up, or on the rocks?" so you know which glass to use. Whew!

Tip-Jar Techniques

Keeping the tip jar full is a science, not an art, and the following little-known tips should help your Bartender-to-Be rake in the big bucks. Make sure he pays attention; a full tip jar can add thousands of dollars a day to his income.

Pours drinks and provides excellent service

Buys customer a round

Laughs at customer's lame jokes

Buys customer a round <u>and</u> laughs at his lame jokes

Practicing The Perfect Pour

Let's face it, anyone can become a bartender. But to achieve the status of a "true Professor of the Bar," your child must not only learn how to take inventory, but also how to pour the perfect drink and create the perfect head on a glass of beer. This, dear parent, is easier said than done, as the accompanying illustrations show.

The Pour: **Fig. 1.** Remove cap from bottle. Pour into glass over ice. **Fig. 2.** The resultant drink after only one month of practice. **Fig. 3.** Perfection! Achieved only after years on the job.

The Head: Fig. 1. Your child's first attempt may look like this. Do not be discouraged. **Fig. 2.** Note the subtle difference after a few weeks of practice. **Fig. 3.** Perfection! Achieved only after years on the job.

Dealing with Others' Expectations

You're bound to have to deal with uppity friends and neighbors who ask you how you could let little Billy spend his life as a bartender instead of going to college. Not to worry. A few smart rejoinders will make them see the error of their ways. When you're done with them, they'll probably take Wendy out of Wellesley and Hank out of Harvard.

When they say:	You'll reply:
"Nice swimming pool. Was it expensive?"	"I figure it was free, based on the money I saved by not buying books for Billy's freshman year."
"I can't believe how much little Wendy's allowance is costing me."	"Little Billy's pulling down sixty thousand dollars a year. He loaned me five hundred dollars yesterday."
"Nice tennis court. Was it expensive?"	"About one year's college tuition."
"Hank pulled another all-nighter to study for his exams."	"Billy slept in till noon again."
"Nice Maybach."	"I'm trading it in; it's got a thousand miles on it."

Raising Your Child to Become a
TV Talk Show Host!

**Degree of Difficulty
2.0**

Oh boy... this is an easy one. You're going to have to make sure your little one can actually ... *talk*! Think you can handle that? If you think your little one got the short end of the stick when it comes to gray matter, not to worry. This super profession doesn't require any skills (except for the aforementioned talking), so it's a pretty easy gig for parents.

So get your child a desk and a few chairs for his playroom, invite some kids from the neighborhood over, and let the interviewing begin!

Cost of Upbringing	Income Potential	Cost/Income Ratio
$$	$$$$$$$	**8.8** (1–10) Higher is better

Have you thought this through? *Points to consider:*	
Pros	**Cons**
Get paid to talk ⟶	Have to listen (sometimes)
Get paid to talk ⟶	Laryngitis
Get to hang out with celebrities ⟶	Get to hang out with wackos
Get to hang out with nudists ⟶	Have to leave your clothes on

Anyone can talk (which is why this is a short chapter). So why doesn't everyone have a talk show? Well, almost everybody does, but only the truly great shows like *Jerry Springer* garner a wide audience.

A better question might be, why in the world would any sane parent want to raise his or her child to be a Talk Show Host? Well, as the above pros and cons show, it ain't a bad gig.

There's talking, and then there's *talking*. Some types are more lucrative than others. After all, customer service representatives talk to people all day long (and actually resolve issues) yet make about 1/100,000,000 of what an average "Host" makes. But customer service reps just talk to average Joes, while your little talker will be schmoozing with important celebrities like Paris Hilton and Dick Cheney. He'll have to learn to fawn over them—laugh at their jokes, be in awe of their acting or singing skills— none of which customer service reps have to learn.

So this is a fairly easy challenge for you as a parent. Your work can be limited to merely selecting the style for the show your little one will ultimately host and teaching him some basic "interviewing" skills. Then just let him yak.

Not much to do here; after all, he'll learn to talk even without your help, so step back. And that extends to babying him, too. Let him cry. He's just looking for attention, and this is good practice for what he'll be doing the rest of his life.

In the crib
• DVD of *Wayne's World*
• Complete twenty-two volume set of *The Tonight Show* with Johnny Carson

Additional furniture
• Desk and multiple chairs for "guests"
• Spotlights on ceiling

On the wall
• Signed autographed photos of Rosie O'Donnell and Garth

The Early Years

Invite all his friends over for cookies and milk and lots of talk. A wide variety of "guests" is recommended, from class president and big-time jock, to cheerleader, class nerd, and class bully. Arguments, fights, and chair-throwing should be encouraged.

Your little one should be warmed up and ready, with microphone in hand, to greet his dad for some "conversation" about his day at the office. This should prepare your kid for the kind of controversial and exciting subject matter he will have to contend with for the rest of his life.

Confrontational, Conversational, or Cozy?

Selecting Their Genre

The key to success is making sure your little one develops a genre all his own. A genre that sets him apart from the rest. Argumentative has been taken. How about a new one: erudite—that has never been tried (but if your kid knows what erudite means, he should aspire to be more than a Talk Show Host).

The easiest style is "canceled," as you can see from the chart below. But it's just too easy and has been chosen in the past by people who should know better—Ricki Lake, for example. In any event, we recommend a completely new genre for a change, like self-depreciating or extremely funny.

Style	Example	Style	Example
Argumentative	Springer	Sarcastic	Ellen
Gossipy	*The View*	Funny	Colbert
Narcissistic	Letterman	Funnier	Stewart
Silly	Leno	Canceled	Montel
Profound	Povich	Canceled	Geraldo
Know it all	Dr. Phil	Canceled	Ricki Lake
Goofy	Kimmel	Canceled	Rosie

159

Home Tutoring

All talk show genres require different "skills;" however, since your child's guests will be selected from the same rotating batch of "celebrities," your Home Tutoring during his early years will simply involve helping him hone his interviewing skills. And not your basic interviewing skills! Successful talk show hosts must perfect the art of the clever and uniquely original opening question. Our examples below are a good place to start. Make your little one practice until he can feign real interest in the answers.

"So tell us about your new movie."
"When did you stop beating your wife?"
"So tell us about your new book."
"Is it true you're dating Paris Hilton?"
"So tell us about your new sitcom."
"What's it like in rehab?"

In Conclusion
A Note from the Institute

We receive may letters from parents who are worried their child won't be able to make it in the highly competitive world of TV Hostdom.

A typical questions is: "Even though my child is convinced she is clever, she has nothing interesting to say and is completely out of touch with what's going on in the world around her. Can she still make it as a host?"

For this type of question, we send a stock letter which basically says, "Maybe not a host, but some sort of sidekick is always a possibility." After all, Andy Rooney is still on the air.

Finally, you may have noted that we have not discussed Oprah. Please be advised, she will be covered in the next edition with her own chapter: God.

TABLOID!

Extra! Extra! Extra!

Rock Star Dates Supermodel!

Celebrity Chef Divorces Beauty Pageant Winner!

Stewardess Marries Prince, Becomes Princess!

Superchild Clustering
The Advantages of Interbreeding

Superchildren tend to "cluster" as they grow up. They interdate and intermarry, which leads to interfighting, intercheating, and interdivorcing.

Much to the delight of the tabloids and the paparazzi.

They date and marry so frequently among themselves, because no matter how well their parents raised them, they grow up so insecure that they need to date someone as famous as they are. This is known in the scientific community as the *I'm famous enough to date someone famous* syndrome.

Chess Master

Of course, not all Superchildren fit the mold. Some grow up more secure (Rocket Scientist), and some are just too nerdy (Chess Master) to date someone as famous as they are. This is known as the *even though you're famous, you still can't get a date* syndrome.

Although scientists generally warn of the dangers of interbreeding, when Superchildren grow up and pro-

161

create, this phenomenon has often turned out to be advantageous.

For some unknown reason, an advantageous Super Trait may be passed on to the next generation, resulting in a new breed of Superchildren even more super! Prime examples are:

Movie Star + Celebrity Chef = Actress who can cook
Supermodel + Chess Master = Model who can think
Flight Attendant + Bestselling Author = Stewardess who can read
Hall of Fame Athlete + Billionaire = Athlete who is not broke at 40

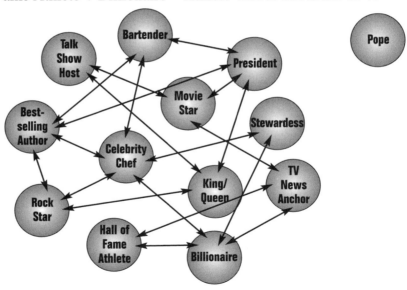

162

Raising the
PerfectChild

Degree of Difficulty
11.0

What is a true Superchild? Pope? President? Nobel Prize Winner? Raising any of them is a piece of cake compared to raising the true Superchild—the near-impossible *Perfectchild*. In fact, it is so difficult that it is beyond the scope of this manual.

A President may have access to the hotline, but the Perfectchild calls his parents once a week. The Pope may be loving, but the Perfectchild is one who does not consider placing his parents in a nursing home when they turn sixty. The Chess Master may be brilliant, but the Perfectchild dutifully completes his homework every night without being asked. The Rock Star may be famous, but the Superchild will never ask you to visit him in rehab.

The Nobel Prize Winner does wonderful things for mankind, but nothing is more wonderful than the Perfectchild who happily asks his aging parents to move in with him.

Cut out this page and affix it to your refrigerator. Every time you find yourself dreaming that your child will grow up to attain the "perfect" profession, dream instead that he or she will grow up to be a caring, thoughtful, loving person. Now *that* would be perfect!

About the Author

To reach their goal of raising a true Superchild, the author's parents assumed that it would be sufficient to buy Ray a cowboy outfit for Christmas when he was six years old. It wasn't, and as a result, he never reached the desired **Saturday Matinee Cowboy TV Star** status.

In her defense, Mr. Strobel's mother commented, "If I had read this book when I was raising Ray, perhaps he wouldn't have turned out to be such a bonehead."

Ray and his wife, Jo, have successsfully raised eight little ones. None reached Superchild status, although five became Supercats and three became Superdogs.

The author, age six

Author's Note

Don't see a suitable Super Profession for *your* Superchild? Not to worry. The author and the directors of the American Superchild Institute are conducting research for Volume II, which will include the following:

- Prima Ballerina • CIA Spy • Chairman of the Fed • Pundit • Oprah
- Pirate • Poet Emeritus • Dali Lama • Bookie • Greek God/Goddess
- Maven • Heart Surgeon • Super Hero • Ghost • Hairdresser to the Stars
- Circus Clown • Guru • Customer Service Representative • and more!

164